7 DAYS TO POWERFUL TEAMS

USING THE EXPERIENCE ORIENTATED MANAGEMENT TECHNIQUE

GARY YARDLEY & JAN KELLY

TIMES BOOKS INTERNATIONAL
Singapore • Kuala Lumpur

This book is dedicated to

Mic Malthouse

for ensuring that champions don't rest within the nest.

This edition was first published in 1996
by Times Books International
an imprint of Times Editions Pte Ltd
Times Centre
1 New Industrial Road
Singapore 536196

Times Subang
Lot 46, Subang Hi-Tech Industrial Park
Batu Tiga
40000 Shah Alam
Selangor Darul Ehsan
Malaysia

Printed in Singapore

ISBN 981 204 651 8

The Challenge

Every experience is a moment that connects us with people, resources and potential. We do not live our lives in isolation. We depend upon others to help us realise our dreams. This is where teams come into their own. The potential of most teams, however, is rarely fulfilled, since there are often many limiting beliefs that hold people back. These include the beliefs that teams are the breeding ground for negative office politics, that individuals will not receive personal recognition for their work and that conflict will be rife.

This book grew out of a challenge to show that teams can be an opportunity to share resources and learn at an expediential rate, given you can learn from other people's experience. We worked with a team from a small computer company which was having difficulty developing new markets. They were a team where ideas clashed and personal egos ran riot.

The work we did with this team included identifying their dysfunctional patterns of behaviour and substituting these patterns with more productive and effective ways of communicating. They were all taught the fundamentals of rapport, and how to ensure that all members receive recognition, respect and reassurance for their contributions. Individual resources were identified in order to increase their value and worth within the team. Team members were also encouraged to generate other possibilities for future development.

The group formed a cohesive, motivated team prepared to focus on the challenges which lay ahead instead of diverting their energies on internal squabbling. There is always a better way of doing things. People just need to be given the chance. We thank them for the opportunity of being part of that transition.

The Challenge

Contents

Chapter 1

Experience Orientated Management (EOM): *Project Potential*

Defining EOM

1. EOM creates better experiences for others, and directs staff's attention, throughout all levels of the organisation, to enriching experiences that make relating with your company the wisest business decision. You will be able to create useful experiences that ensure opportunities thrive.
2. EOM assists people to become more experienced, so that they may better utilise information around them. Managers who can influence others and create a tomorrow that is based on fulfilment and enjoyment will be successful in utilising the potential of their teams.

Every company has projects that are either part of the mainline business or run parallel in a supportive way. These projects enable the company to be successful. By achieving the objectives of a project, we add substance to the way we do business.

Every project has an end in sight. The journey towards that end should be planned and well thought through. Knowing what we want and what we need gives us a set of parameters where our outcome is identified and a criteria for success established. In other words, this gives us a destination that each member of the team is working towards. Along the way there may be many distractions or surprises which can be incorporated or ignored, so that they do not detract from the project's conclusion.

The dilemma of management in the '70s and '80s was whether to develop the potential of the individual or the team, since conflict can arise when the needs of the team are at variance with the needs and personal fulfilment of the individual. The way of the future strongly indicates that individuals need to be self-managed, so that they can come together for projects that require not only their specific skills, but also the opportunity to stretch their personal potential. The role of managing teams in the future will be developing and building relationships and understanding and monitoring the dynamics that teams can create, to extract the full potential which each member brings to the team.

ABSTRACTION

Team managers create a reality for others. They take an idea, based on what is needed, and forecast possibilities. From this *abstract* the project is born. Throughout the project, what will matter is the relationships between people, the group dynamics and the sharing of skills and ideas. Team members make connections between the work they are doing and the learning they can gain from these projects. Tasks are allocated so that there is an interdependence between individuals who rely upon each other's ability and expertise. The group can invariably achieve more than an individual. Therefore, being a member of a team allows us to abstract a sense of belonging and worth for the contributions that we make.

How the manager approaches the variety of possible abstractions available, along with how the journey is constructed, will determine the team's rewards. Relationships are built upon many experiences. The more experienced the relationships, the more individuals can strive together to meet the challenges, and work towards a shared vision and a greater return. By constantly searching for ideas that will give greater possibilities, the team remains dynamic and flexible, as its members move towards their goals.

CONSTRUCTION

The team leader needs to *construct* a direction that will keep team members focused and 'on task' so that individuals do not lose sight of the 'bigger picture' or their reason for working together. Specific applications of the work being produced need to be highlighted or reinforced so that learning is accelerated and team members develop a sense of progression and achievement.

With the destination or outcome of the project clearly in sight, managers therefore construct a plausible way to achieve success, examining the challenges or difficulties that may be encountered, together with the resources and individual skills that can be utilised. Details and specific tasks need to be identified, with a pragmatic course of action thoroughly planned. By doing this, time and energy are not wasted, and each moment can be more fully utilised, so that the final outcome is achieved expediently.

Managers need to ascertain the probable reality for a successful project. Preparation will include costing, planning relationships and determining which experiences will be valuable for team members to have. When constructing a plausible reality of success, organising of resources, skills and information is crucial.

EXTRACTION

Planning for all contingencies allows the manager to *extract* the potential of all team members, so that performing as a coherent team becomes a rewarding and challenging experience. Individuals can extract the experiences which give their lives substance. As a team member, we can extract fresh ideas, new products and services, learning and additional skills which we gain from the experiences and suggestions of those around us. All of these ideas we can refine so that we continually and consistently become better at what we do. We can also experience a sense of involvement by supporting each other, particularly when the going gets tough. We can have a place where we belong, where we share information generously instead of rigidly protecting what is ours.

These relationships allow us to experience our reality as a joint venture into the unknown. The potential of our workers and of our business will be measured by a product and service which is profitable for all involved. Our beliefs and personal style can make this happen.

It is this constant search for new possibilities and better ways of constructing experiences that sustains a team and maintains a

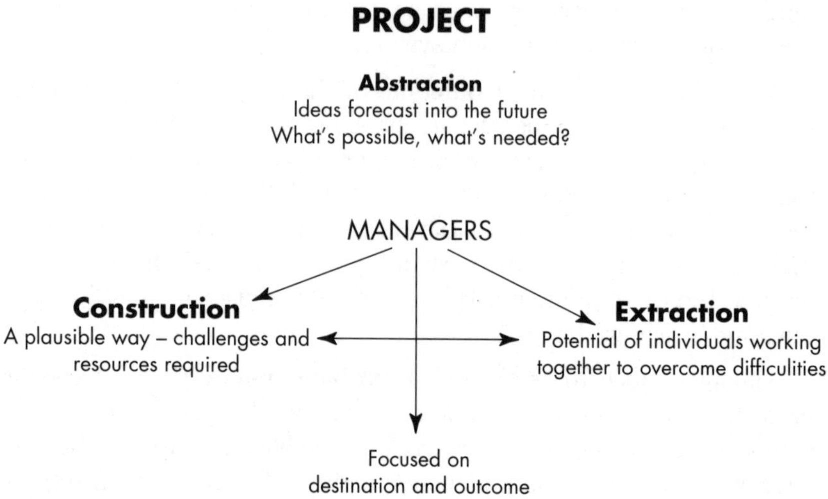

successful company. Team members will give feedback on what is useful by extracting meaning from their experiences. As managers, we need to involve everyone in the process because their perceptions are important. Employees need a say in refining the delivery of the project, so that they can believe in it. This then allows them to sell it to others.

The idea has to be sufficiently worked through to identify an abstract which is important enough to warrant the investment of time, money and human resources. Regardless of the project being undertaken, focus must now be directed towards constructing the reality and creating what is plausible, to extract the potential of the team. This allows members to arrive at the destination. As the project unfolds the abstract takes greater shape. It begins to take on more form as people become more involved in the pursuit of reaching for what was deemed possible.

MOMENT MANAGEMENT

The skill for managers comes in determining what is required and by whom. Getting the most out of others means that we have to be focused on what we want. If we are to lead individuals who are self-managed and assist them in becoming more so, we need to be able to rise above the moment, to manage the relationships and the experiences.

For teams and individuals to perform to their potential, managers have to let go of being responsible for every moment. Allow others to take charge of the moment, or else the moment takes on a greater significance than warranted. When this occurs we can often lose sight of our destination because we are distracted by minor obstacles and irritations. They become important as we respond and react, rather than move forward. Don't get sidetracked by the moment. It is too easy to get lost in the power and control of just managing problems. It takes many moments to complete a project, and one is not more important than another.

When we encourage individuals to be self-managed many of the activities that consume our day will become redundant. Some of these include:

- Motivating people
- Checking up on individuals
- Disciplining employees
- Attending an endless array of meetings
- Organising tasks and procedures
- Solving the constant stream of daily problems presented to management, i.e. putting out fires

Most of these chores are repeated every day. When people become self-managed all of these processes will no longer be necessary. There will be no need for the project 'police person'.

Experiences are made up of many moments, and relationships are made up of many experiences. Elegant team management directs and facilitates individuals to reach their potential and overcome their difficulties by utilising their own resources. This, of course, is a developmental issue. For instance, for the last 20 to 30 years people have been faced with a barrage of books, tapes and information on how to manage. However, we have now reached the point where we have enough education to go to the next step. We have to 'chunk up' and go for the larger experience, that is, to manage ourselves. People who are not interested in taking personal responsibility for chores, being accountable and standing up for themselves will be left behind.

The moment is seductive because we have control and power. We become the all knowing and all doing. It feels good to be the resident problem-solver. When we become someone's solution we only reinforce their problem, their passivity and their dependence. We also know that these moments will be repeated many times because we have taught people that this is the most immediate way they can connect with us. Our managing style in the past has taught them this. While these moments of power and control will occur in the future, remember that these situations are not about learning, growing and building another's potential. They are not about taking the future head-on. They merely keep us stuck in the moment.

Managing the moments = *Context*
Deals with issues and problems

Managing the experiences = *Structure*
Focuses on potential resources

Managing the relationships = *Process*
Keeps the end in sight

Functional managers are able to move between the 3 levels

The only thing we can guarantee when working in teams is that we will have relationships and experiences. Because of this, experienced managers are worth their weight in gold. They can translate a vision and dream into action. They know *how* to direct, *when* to direct, *why* to direct, *who* to direct and *what* is important for each worker in order for the project to be completed expediently and thoroughly.

If we begin to manage the experience, we start to extend ourselves forward in time, anticipating the way toward completion of the project.

Energy is directed towards structuring experiences that capture the imagination and take people beyond the moment. This opens up a realm of possibilities for a manager to begin the real process of managing. This process involves setting challenges and giving parameters for others to work within. This enables individuals to achieve a form of success which has them involved and responsible for their own personal achievements, as well as reaching the project's outcome.

While team leaders will manage the moment as well as the experience, they can also take it a step further by managing the relationships which are occurring within the team. Managers need to set the pace by noticing how members interact, how they combine to complement each other, and how they generate what is required. Creating and building relationships of substance can truly create something which is dynamic and exciting, so that together people work towards a shared goal.

In putting together a team or selecting an individual for a project we have to ask questions that focus on what is required and what is essential. We have to take risks as managers, based on what is plausible. Out of this we need evidence which will back up our predictions. This makes us accountable, not only for our selections, but where we take our teams.

Once we have identified our destination, we can work backwards by examining what relationships and experiences will be required to assist and facilitate the team in reaching their targets. By doing this, we can predict the likely problems and the moments that will challenge the team and their project.

When problems occur, we have the choice of intervening, but more importantly, we can prepare and manage these distractions before they occur. In most projects there will be unexpected developments. This is where our energy and time will be required, not in the moment. As a manager we need to free ourselves so our skills can be more effectively used when required. This is the contingency of a successful completion of the project.

Chapter 2

Functional Teams

With families, groups and teams we create dynamics. When these dynamics work well the team will collectively outperform individuals. These same teams can also cause an amazing amount of destruction. Our role as managers is to direct and orientate people to other possibilities and to assist and guide them out of dysfunctional and disruptive behaviour. The following are common patterns that occur when power and control become the intention of influence.

DYSFUNCTIONAL DYNAMICS

Dynamics within a group become dysfunctional when team members, for the majority of the time, are not in touch with their resources. Games of power and control will be evident, and personal growth and development is kept to a minimum. While the project may still get completed, it does not progress expediently. Conflict between team members will predominate, with behaviours ranging from passive dependence, active resistance to the objectives of the group and a reluctance to accept personal responsibility for the events which are occurring. The three major stances of dysfunctional dynamics include:

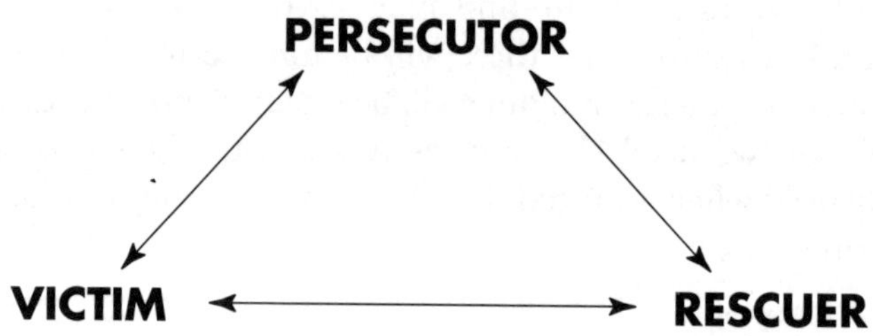

Each of these patterns are interactive. That is, they need each other to survive, to maintain individual roles and keep the group intact. These roles can have a positive function in specific situations. It is only when they dominate our way of responding and coping with stress that they become detrimental and counter-productive for individuals and their relationships.

The Persecutor

This is usually the easiest to identify because invariably the persecutor is the loudest and most vocal person in the team. This pattern tends to be overbearing, since individuals focus on their rights and others' 'wrongs'. While they would describe their behaviour as appropriate, good and successful, they see others' behaviour as inappropriate or lacking in competence. The persecutor's intentions are often to want more for others, by pointing out mistakes to increase learning. Their failing, however, is in their style and approach to those around them. They can be too direct, and generally lack patience and consideration for people who perceive the world differently.

The persecutor has many variations in behaviour, and can sometimes hide in more acceptable patterns, depending on the situation. Clues to this behaviour occur when people are under stress from an external source, and will include the following behaviour:

- Being cynical/sarcastic
- Being catty, feeling superior
- Backstabbing
- Belittling others
- Blaming others and pointing fingers
- Being correct and right all the time

In dealing with a persecutor, it is best to agree with them in principle, to reduce the need for them to defend a position or attack to save face. By pacing their experience, we can then lead them to points of difference, by agreeing to disagree. Give them another orientation, and fulfil their basic need for validation. These individuals will need assistance and understanding in:

1. Perceiving the world differently, and appreciating that others can have a different perspective. All perspectives are valid; there will always be more than one way. Allow others to have their own personal style. Rapport skills will assist in this process.
2. Building flexibility and choice, so the individual is faced with more than one option. Generate alternative points of view, so that their perspective is less rigid.
3. Being more indirect in their approach. They need to soften their tone of voice, and ask questions rather than give commands. Be aware of others' preferences. It will be more useful to influence or persuade others rather than dominate and put them down.
4. Working with the individual on their frustration, irritation and anger to become more discerning with their emotional responses. Often these individuals are quick to become agitated. Ironically, this response has less of an impact on other team members because people generally get used to frequent, strong emotions.
5. Developing a more accommodating image, since these individuals are often seen as the 'bully'. The importance of tight deadlines needs to be reduced, while mistakes by others should be seen as a learning opportunity for everyone.
6. Making more useful decisions in relation to others, based on their individual competencies and abilities. Expectations of others need to be clearly stipulated to reduce confusion.

Every now and again it is all right to complain. It helps us to let off steam, but also shows us that we are not in charge of the situation. Therefore, resorting to persecuting behaviours too frequently will signal that it is time to address some issues, or learn new strategies in coping with external demands and pressures.

Remember, if we listen closely, conversations will tell us more about the individual speaking than the person being described! When we persecute, we ultimately persecute ourselves, because we offend and distance others quickly. Instead, find a new balance in every situation, before reacting and responding.

The Victim

The victim is the most passive of all stances. The victim takes a 'one down' position. It is a lonely position, characterised by having no say, taking the "Who'd listen to me", "What's the point, nothing will change" attitude. These individuals feel powerless in any adversity or challenge, and see themselves as scapegoats. They are easily intimidated, frightened or coerced. They see themselves as being in an unfair position, and require support and energy. Life is unjust and they have enough evidence to support this view. They need other people to give directions as an external focus or control. They can subjugate their own feelings and put others before themselves. This generates feelings of martyrdom or guilt. They do not want to offend or upset.

There are many variations of how the victim operates and functions. Some of these are genuine circumstances, such as economic and environmental disasters. However, other variations include:

- Accepting responsibility to reduce tension.
- Self-defeating and destructive habits.
- Being helpless and hopeless in situations.
- Running around after people, being 'the worrier'.
- Being quiet as a mouse, with nothing worthwhile to say.
- Being the whipping boy.

All these behaviours are a way of managing external tension and reducing a perceived or real threat. At times, it is useful to reduce tension. However, when these strategies become a way of negating challenges or difficulties through self-depreciation, they are no longer valid. A victim predicts things that are going to be terrible, plan for disaster and in some cases, becomes the disaster.

Management of these people requires that they avoid persecutors. Instead, give these individuals more challenges. Give clear expectations of what is required, and how they can go about achieving these requirements. Tolerate excuses less, and point out what is useful in their behaviour. These individuals will require assistance and understanding in:

1. Being encouraged to be themselves and to think in different ways without offending other people. Also reinforce and affirm that their views have validity and are important.
2. Identifying other aspects and personal qualities that they have, and showing them how to use these. Connect them with their resources and demonstrate how to get support in a direct way.
3. Being more direct in expressing their needs to others, rather than waiting for others to fulfil them. When these individuals become more assertive, they will no longer have to apologise for their requests or expectations.
4. Connecting them with their hopes and dreams, and building a step-by-step approach to personal achievement, detailing what they have to do along the way.
5. Working on their image, and the worthwhile abilities they have to offer. They need to like and enjoy the many facets of themselves that make their contribution unique. Teach them how to be kind to themselves, to relax and pamper themselves.
6. Give them a cause which is greater than themselves. If they're going to put in a lot of their time and energy, let them do it for a greater cause. Explore a variety of perspectives and build different meanings.

When things go wrong, the victim is invariably at the centre of the difficulty. They tend to have a miserable life, and bring misery wherever they go. They seek out the status quo, by just coping and surviving.

The Rescuer

The rescuer is a champion for other people's causes. They are always on the lookout for crusades and causes to work on. Their positive intention is that they don't like unfairness or injustice. The more nebulous intention is that they want to solve other people's problems as a way of meeting their own needs. There are many subtle forms of how the rescuer works:

- The do gooder

- The saint/saviour
- The old dependable
- The deflector
- The arranger
- The righteous

It is important that we are involved in relationships and in assisting others. We have to remain alert that we do not become intrusive in people's lives. Consider whose needs and beliefs are really being served.

Managers have to be careful they don't find themselves being sucked into the rescue position. When we rescue we deny individuals the ability to adapt and survive for themselves. This only builds dependency. It may be important, however, to become involved for short-term and immediate crisis situations. When the crisis has subsided, back off to allow other people to grow from their own experiences. The rescuer is a 'busybody' who believes they know what's best for other people. These individuals will require assistance and understanding in:

1. Differentiating between direct intervention, and standing back to allow others to explore and learn from their experiences. Identify what the other person may lose because of the rescuing behaviour.
2. Identifying the difference between another's issue and their own personal agenda. It may be their own concerns and worries which are motivating their behaviour, not the person they are attempting to assist.
3. Seeing the larger perspective, to differentiate between now, future and past situations. Perceive the system rather than the problem, and examine what processes may be currently fuelling the issue.
4. Interpreting issues and concerns differently. Have these individuals acknowledge alternative points of view. Find new meanings and situations of how useful each experience is, so that learning and growth occurs for all concerned.

5. Thinking of strategies that are relevant and tailored for others, to assist and promote interdependence. Generate ways of how this person can empower others, rather than their current behaviour.

6. Recognising how they can empower themselves without solving the dilemmas of others. Also consider other strategies for giving themselves respect and reassurance, when they communicate with other team members.

To rescue presupposes that somebody actually needs to be saved. We can engage in this behaviour if we choose, but only after we have received a direct request for this type of assistance. However, in responding to any request, consider the implications and the repercussions of any intervention. Choosing not to be involved can mean walking away from commitment to other people. It is how we intervene which is the key. Allow other people to be in charge of their lives, and be wary of repetitive patterns in another's difficulties. To be an expert in problems is a problem that needs to be resolved!

Each of these dysfunctional positions are interchangeable and roles can change rapidly. For instance, the rescuer aligns with the victim. Together they can persecute the persecutor, who then becomes the victim, and is invariably rescued by the previous victim. When these two come together, they tend to persecute the rescuer. The more the system is allowed to continue, the more crazy it becomes; intertwining and interweaving!

In family systems, these dynamics will move quickly as relationships become closer and more intense, since the issues are more likely to be fuelled by emotions, with individuals less afraid of having their say. In business, these patterns are more likely to be subtle and slower to develop, since relationships are not as intense, and are fuelled more by logic and strategies. Both are about individual control and power, and are based on positions of manipulation rather than influence patterns.

All relationships are dynamic. We need to extract the useful components of each of these situations. We can challenge the beliefs and values that we have about each pattern. In doing so, we can at one attitude and style, and decide whether we want to be hooked into a system where the dynamics are dysfunctional.

FUNCTIONAL DYNAMICS

Teams provide an excellent opportunity for people to work together in a way that accelerates individual learning. Being part of a team can give us a place where we belong, relationships which have substance, a position where we feel valued and important, and experiences rich in possibilities. Teams can function in the most exciting way when conflicts are considered a challenge, individuals take responsibility for their actions, different options are constantly generated, and members support each other to produce a project not achievable by the individual alone. The three major stances of functional dynamics include:

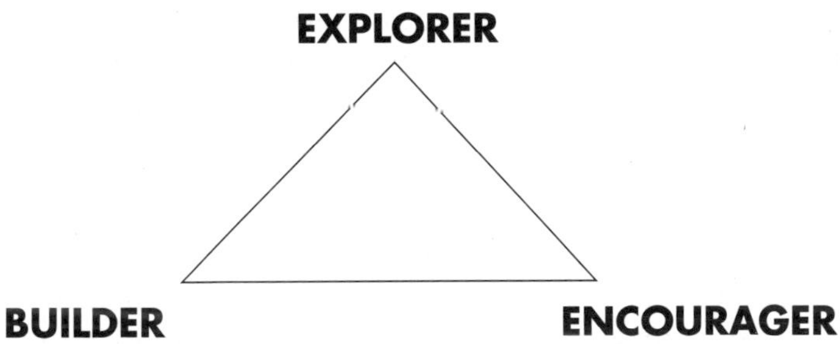

The Explorer

The explorer is someone who recognises possibilities and potential. They are on a quest for answers. They are therefore constantly asking questions, such as "What if?", "What might be?", "What could be?" These people actively seek out what else there is; not happy to accept what currently exists; there must be more. They sort for differences in the world around them, and move away from those things which are similar. They actively move outside their areas of comfort. They will create a vision, then find ways to reach it. They also build the connections and associations necessary for others to follow. In business, they are the entrepreneurs. They are the leaders into the unknown. They believe in what is possible, and back it up with their actions.

Explorers respect those around them who challenge themselves to strive for something unique. They enjoy most things which are creative, and are in awe of how others come to understand something new, regardless of the endeavour. By venturing into unknown territory they create adventure. They are single-minded and tenacious in the pursuit of their dreams. Unlike dreamers, they take action. They are not happy with mediocre or safe answers.

These people are internally driven towards a compelling future. They reassure others by backing up projects and adventures and being supportive and encouraging. They search for the elusive. If they are good explorers they mark out their territory as they go. In other words, they want others to follow, to be able to find what they have found.

Their weaknesses, however, are that they get too involved in the project and sometimes their ideas can be too outrageous. These people are best managed by giving them more than one project at a time, and by making them accountable and responsible for their progress. They usually have difficulty relating to accountants, conservatives and staid managers.

The Builder

The builder recognises a project for its construction. They enjoy following specifications, guidelines and plans. They require something solid to work from and enjoy creating something of beauty. They enjoy the challenge of doing something, and are happy to work things through to their conclusion. They recognise how things work and can quickly adapt from a given plan. They are focused on the end use, its applications and implementations. They respect a plan and its specifications, and more importantly, its details.

The builder knows how to work with resources and do what is required. They are clear about how things can be done, stresses and strains likely to be involved, and how to calculate the costs of the project. They have an understanding of the resources they would like, but also respect the alternatives. They will admire others who can work with the details and intricacies of constructing something of substance. When constructing a project they become the craftsman, whose honour is at stake if the project is delivered in a sloppy fashion.

They are intrigued by the finishes they can produce. Their performance and standard is high, and they like to build things that stand the test of time. They take responsibility and accountability right to the end.

Their weakness is that they can become caught up in the intricacies and details of a project. They need to be directed towards the end of the project, and involved in delegating and facilitating others. They relate well to all aspects of the business, but can be hard and tough, since they place high expectations on themselves and those around them.

The Encourager

The encourager recognises a passion, a belief and a possibility. They may not have all the answers to the questions asked, but they have the desire for others to accomplish more. They therefore offer support whenever they can. They are also able to spot a good idea and its potential. They recognise qualities and traits in others, they perceive most things in a constructive way and find a use for this in every situation. They respect learning and personal endeavours. They admire the courage of others, and feel compelled to support it.

They will see and respect the positive intentions of others, and will back up their intuitions of people. They are not easily disheartened and continue to sort for options and choices. They notice differences in individuals and in groups. They value information and knowledge as vital resources which people need. They give reassurance through their actions, which are continually supportive. They stand by people, particularly when the going becomes difficult. They are champions of causes, especially when they see the purpose behind the idea. The encourager seeks out relevant and useful information, and will offer suggestions readily. Their weakness is that they tend to put their own needs aside and are most content when others accomplish. They therefore can place too much faith in others. However, as long as they can extract the learning from this, they can be encouraged by the experience. They make ideal team players as they act as a backstop for others. Their real skill lies in facilitation and bringing out the best that others can produce.

These three functional roles combined can produce a powerful team. They can tackle just about anything, particularly if they are supplied with the resources, knowledge and equipment. The explorer needs to seek out new ways or other options and possibilities for things to be done differently. The builder needs to construct, and put together these ideas to create substance. This role gives a framework for others to relate to. The encourager needs to support both the explorer and the builder through difficult times and when progress is laborious. Therefore, the explorer paves the way for the builder to construct something, with the encourager being supportive and attentive to the needs of others. As a simple philosophy or set of dynamics in a company, these are the ingredients that make a relationship, a team and a company dynamic.

Each of us will have our projects which need to be explored. We can get encouragement and back up from those around us, and build something together. Ultimately as managers, we have to demonstrate all three positions, and as the group develops, it will be more useful to move to the position of encourager.

Rather than compete against team members, we can assist others in building their dreams. These stances are not looking for what doesn't work, or for problems that have to be solved. They are focused on the answers to the questions that have yet to be asked. All functional positions take an interest in how things work and function, and how things can happen and be created. This is their purpose.

Chapter 3

Challenging Managers' Beliefs

Each of us have beliefs, and these beliefs help construct our reality. The question is, what do we know about them? The more we know about our beliefs, the more we can understand how they influence our behaviour. It may be that some beliefs are not useful, in which case we can shift or use them less. Similarly, we will have beliefs which are productive and stimulating. These beliefs we would want to use more fully.

We know that beliefs are powerful because they allow us to do some things and not others. They become the parameters of what we believe is possible. Beliefs are not good or bad, or right or wrong, however, they are our way of making sense of and interpreting the world, so that it has meaning and substance.

Our beliefs can limit or enhance our projects. Those beliefs that limit us are the ones that take us further away from our destination, or allow us to become stuck in the moment, over a point or issue. Those beliefs that enhance our work take us closer to our destination and create an experience that propels us forward into the future.

We cannot, however, perceive beliefs as just limiting or enhancing, since each belief has the components of both. The skilful manager works with these components, rather than trying to change another's beliefs. Managing is about believing in people, and also acknowledging what they believe in. During a project every member will have their beliefs altered in some way because we are influenced by those around us. So rather than changing counter productive beliefs, we can work with what we have and what already exists within the team.

We have to develop and direct our own beliefs, and those of our team members, so that by the conclusion of the project we have personally learned a great deal, and also added to someone else's belief system, rather than subtracted from it. The last thing we want is for everybody to be the same. Similarly, we do not want clashes between individuals because of contrasting beliefs, since these create distractions, conflict and moments which we need to manage.

Individuals will always bring their own beliefs to the team. They are vital in adding to the body of resources needed to have the project completed. Invariably, these beliefs don't work in isolation, but within a system of other beliefs, with one or two predominating and overriding the rest. In putting together a team, we have to determine what these overriding beliefs will be for they create the limitations of achieving what's probable.

These overriding beliefs are fundamental to every project. They need to be identified and agreed upon, from the beginning of the project. These central beliefs are less open to change, but they can develop as the project unfolds. For instance, what beliefs do team members have about the project's destination? This belief will influence individual performance and personal motivation towards the task.

Overriding beliefs will include a belief in the outcome, believing in the people involved, and believing in the purpose. These set up the guidelines which allow individuals to work together to create a shared reality that allows them to achieve their goals and be committed to the fundamental beliefs of the project. Once these are established it gives the manager a reference point to refer back to. As a manager, it is important to determine, for each member of the team, the beliefs behind the questions which we most commonly ask:

1. Are we getting closer to what we want?
2. What value do we place on what other members offer?
3. What is the greater reason for doing this project or task?

Most of the issues that can disrupt a team will come from the responses to these three questions. They can bind and blend people together to achieve amazing things. Alternatively, they can distract individuals from the task at hand, and create divergent behaviours that will act as stumbling blocks for the team to successfully complete its project. It is crucial to remember that when we are part of a team and endeavour to overcome issues, difficulties and problems, we have to have something larger to reach for, other than our own likes or dislikes.

What will be more useful is to examine our beliefs, to determine which ones enhance our potential, and which ones limit our behaviour. It will be these beliefs that determine the performance of the team and the problems which will be highlighted. By placing our beliefs and those of our team members under the microscope for self-examination, we can begin to identify which beliefs will inadvertently influence what is probable for the team to achieve.

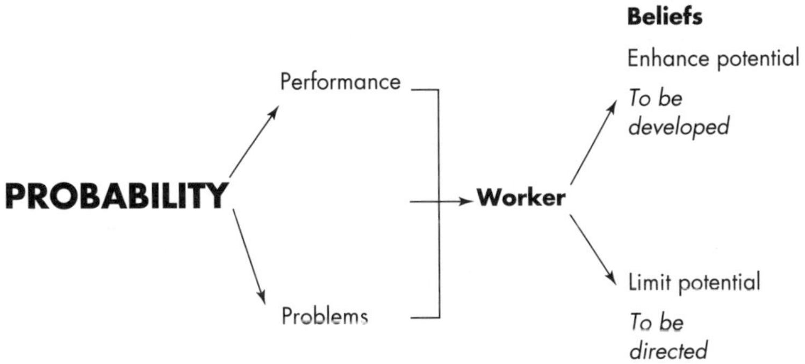

We need to assist individuals and relationships to be flexible, so that they can cope when their beliefs are challenged. Rather than changing or dismissing another's experience, we can develop the beliefs they have so that they enhance their own potential. We can also direct their beliefs to those things they have yet to discover.

Developing Beliefs

The beliefs we had five years ago are not the same as the ones we have today. Therefore, we can assume that the beliefs we will have in five years' time will also be different. The only time we are directly faced with a belief is when it is no longer useful or when it does not allow us to achieve the things we want. These are the beliefs we need to look at more closely, and update if necessary.

Personal development is about finding tomorrow's beliefs and using them today. Very few of us actually plan for our new beliefs. We have goals and targets for what we want to strive towards. These may include beliefs about what we want to own or possess, skills and knowledge we wish to develop, and relationships we want to pursue. However, we rarely consider what our beliefs of tomorrow will be.

In addition, if we do think about the beliefs we wish to develop and use in our future, we may also want to consider how these beliefs will influence and fill the moment. For instance, if we have a belief of "I can't do this", then this will be so. If, however, we were to develop this belief and explore "What parts can I do?" or "Who can assist me with what I currently can't do?" or "What is it that I can learn?" then we are beginning to develop possibilities, so that some time in the future we can look back and say "It was easy!"

When we are managing others and directing a team or project, we are also developing the beliefs of our team members. Begin by creating the realm of what's plausible. Any work that people do has to make sense to them. It has to be a natural continuation of who they are. The importance of managing successfully is to develop the beliefs of those around us. When we do this we enhance another's potential because their beliefs allow them to believe that they are capable of doing more; that more is always possible.

Directing Beliefs

When we manage others we will be exposed to beliefs or parts of a belief that limit another's experience and relationships. In these instances, it is worthwhile to direct their belief to a more functional understanding and a different way of achieving their targets and dreams. We need to show them how their beliefs can be a self-imposed limitation which influences their behaviour. Identify the effects that these beliefs create, and begin to direct them to more choices and other options that this same belief will allow them to consider.

Too many people defend beliefs with a vigour and tenacity that outweighs the importance of the belief. At times, individuals can demonstrate a certainty that the belief doesn't deserve. Believing in ourselves and those around us is an ongoing process that has no room for personal stands which limit our relationships and experiences and restrict our development. When we make a stand because of an outdated belief which is no longer useful, not only does the belief become redundant, so does the person utilising it. Generation after generation we have been shown this lesson. In fact, those that work with the future are predicting and observing how beliefs will develop and what direction they will take. These individuals know that to change a market is harder than to develop it.

EXCUSES

One of the major factors which will hold us back as managers are the excuses we give ourselves and others to describe our work performance. Similarly, the excuses that we accept from our team members can also hold them back from growing at their optimum rate. Each of us has to excuse ourselves from doing some things, mainly because there are so many things to do. For most of us, we become skilful in building plausible excuses that are reasonable to others, and to ourselves. The majority of people tend to use excuses to justify their current actions rather than accept the feedback they receive as an opportunity to do things better in the future.

The advantage of excuses is that they allow us to get on with other things. The disadvantage is that they can stop us from doing what we have to do. Excuses tend to evolve around our behaviour, when we rationalise our actions. Mostly, they allow us to save face when we have made an error in judgement.

The Structure of Excuses

Adults use excuses to explain their behaviour, and to demonstrate their preferences and prejudices. As such, excuses are neither good nor bad, but an opportunity to recognise people's limitations, and more importantly, what matters to them. However, since most of us want to be seen as understanding by others, we tend to accept excuses when we believe they are reasonable. All excuses will have a rationale and a justification which will allow us to defend our current position:

The excuse	*What*	"I'm too tired to do it."
The rationale	*Why*	"I've been working all day."
The justification	*Rights*	"I deserve a rest."

Most difficulties begin to occur between individuals when we present our rationale behind the excuse. People tend to disagree between what's relevant and useful because of their different perspectives. At this point, reframing or presenting another point of view becomes a powerful tool. However, when individuals move directly into justification we now have the beginning of a stand-off, because people will always defend their rights.

In such a situation, respecting their territory will reduce the impasse. The best way of dealing with this is to lead by example. Leaders will get other people to do things by going first and reassuring others that more possibilities are available to them. Therefore, flexibility of our own behaviour becomes paramount if we are to challenge our own beliefs successfully, while expecting other team members to do the same.

We use excuses to build reassurance for our behaviour. This can be effective at times in reducing our levels of stress. However, if we are not careful, we can use excuses to camouflage our incompetence. Generally this is transparent to other team members and colleagues. We can analyse our excuses to identify where we may need to do some extra work in our own development to become more effective as a manager.

This self-analysis is also an opportunity to show other members of the team that we are not afraid to take on the challenge and identify those excuses that perhaps we have hidden behind in the past. We can begin by noting the excuses which we more commonly use, and ascertain the rationale and justification which supports them. We have to be extremely careful not to justify our justifications, particularly over another's point of view. Instead, begin to build a compromise or common ground, so that people can explore new behaviour.

It is preferable not to reach a stand-off on justifications and personal rights. People will defend these at all costs, and since most individuals have invested a great deal in the team, they are less likely to walk away; rather they will stand their ground and defend vigorously. And so begins the struggle to build substance within a relationship, by what we are prepared to give and take. As managers, we should remain clear on our rules regarding:

- Appropriate expectations
- Feedback on unrealistic expectations
- Priorities of what is important
- Taking responsibility for mistakes made
- Jeopardising the team's success
- Defending personal egos
- Useful and relevant excuses

Excuses can stop us from doing our best. They will be based on our expectations, which presumably are different to those around us. Sadly, if we excuse ourselves long enough, we eventually come to believe that the behaviour was never a possibility. So invariably our excuses provide us with a safety net.

Unfortunately, our excuses most often occur when we have let other people down. So we have to be aware of the effect that our excuses have on others. Our impact may not have been what we intended, and if the cycle continues unchecked, we may inadvertently gain a reputation of being unreliable. Generally, we never have to challenge the majority of our excuses. It is only when they come into conflict with ourselves and others frequently, that we may want to take a closer look.

Rather than automatically delivering an excuse, we have to remember that we are part of a team. This allows us to put more substance into our work and into our relationships. We can connect with passion so that we are committed to the task at hand, and to the people involved and they are committed to us. At times we may experience confusion as our reality is challenged. There is our reality and there is the reality of the other members in the team. This confusion lets us know that we are in a space of new learning. It is an opportunity to learn how to cope and adapt. It is exciting when we meet someone for the first time because we can learn about all the things that this person brings to the team. The more important and closer this person becomes to us, the more we have to relate to them. We can't avoid it. Nor would we want to!

As team leaders we need to highlight areas of learning, so that all individuals can learn from each other's mistakes or confusion. We also need to assist others in being supportive to those around them, so that all individuals can take an active interest in the development of the team. Support and encouragement are particularly crucial during the middle stages of any project, since this is the most likely time when enthusiasm for the task may waver.

Excuses are fundamental to our integrity, and are mostly seen as negative because they are used to defend territory and behaviour rather than open up alternatives. We need to be accountable for our actions. It is a healthy process to recognise and admit our limitations so that we can begin to seek assistance from others, to eventually excuse ourselves less in the future.

Chapter 4

Leadership

We are surrounded by thousands of leaders who are older and more experienced than us. However, as every parent knows, not all children will follow. And after a while we can begin to wonder who is really leading who? In reality, we all lead. We lead our own lives, while the people we meet and the events we experience will influence what we decide to follow. It is always our decision what we choose to follow, or what we choose to oppose and stand our ground on.

There is of course safety in following the majority. We have a shared reality and a consensual sense of normality. This has been proven in economics, business, politics and societies. While we can make mistakes, it does not seem so bad when we make them en masse. We also tend to persecute those who don't conform because these individuals threaten our reality. It is possible for these people to prove themselves by creating a credible alternative, but swimming against the stream can be a struggle.

Each of us has a potential to do great things in our lives and also influence those around us. Sooner or later, someone will look to us to be the lead. This can be done even in the smallest of way. For instance, being the first to say hello is taking the lead. This has opened many doors, begun most relationships and created numerous opportunities. There are, however, people who have difficulty saying hello, and will wait until others go first. The more they do this, the more difficult that one word becomes. When we take the lead we are required to take a risk without our outcome being guaranteed. That's what life is about.

Leadership presupposes that there is somewhere to go or an objective which can be achieved. It also requires individuals who will follow, for without followers leadership becomes meaningless. Napoleon would not have created history without his army. Effective leadership is having others follow our directives. There are many reasons why people play follow-the-leader. It could be a desire to achieve, an opportunity to learn, a chance to be part of something special, a good career move or even perhaps because there is nothing better to do! Whatever the reason, people follow others.

We all need a sense of progress. Doing nothing becomes boring, and adds nothing to our existence. Therefore, life becomes repetitive or meaningless. Success is the challenge that most of us strive for. However, our collective personal history is full of incidents and experiences where failure has set us back. Hopefully we can learn from these experiences by re-thinking and relating to the world in a different way. As leaders, we will make mistakes. These are the moments where we are faced with the challenge of what to do in the next moment. We can more easily live with our mistakes by designing new ways to respond in the future. When we learn from our mistakes it becomes easier for others to follow, since we are continually getting better at what we do.

When faced with failure most of us are left with a loss of personal confidence in our own ability. We tend to question our future decisions and create uncertainty for ourselves at the next challenge. There can also be a loss of confidence from the people who follow our directives. We forget that our greatest learning occurs at the moment when we have the realisation and understanding of the other factors which were not previously considered when we made our decision. Therefore, being a leader exposes us to criticism. This can be healthy if it is an ongoing process of feedback, rather than one of hindsight. The "I told you so" rebuke never helped anyone to learn.

"Success breeds success" is a fallacy. Instead, success breeds followers because people like to share in the achievement and accomplishment of overcoming a challenge. We all like that sense of satisfaction in concluding any endeavour. Striving to achieve a set standard is easy, invariably the challenge comes in setting the standard which will allow us to be successful. Following the trends can also be easy, but creating new enterprises and standards is where the real excitement lies.

Leaders are individuals who go first, but who put themselves second in order to get the most from the whole group. Leadership requires that people put their faith in another, and that they trust this relationship. Faith is a belief with no evidence to support it, while trust is a belief which has supporting evidence. The leader stipulates the standards required for effective and successful productivity. As leaders, when we determine this standard we take a risk, and the greater the risk, the greater the reward and loss. We all know there are opportunities out there, because everyone has a story of "If only I had done this." Well, we didn't take the risk and we missed the opportunity.

Ironically, the safest thing to do in life is to do something entirely different, because then there is no previous standard by which others can judge us. Others can then only do better, or talk about it. People are always waiting and looking out for something that is different. With difference comes interest, intrigue and excitement. The more unique the challenge, the easier it is because we don't have to follow other people's mistakes or outdated beliefs. We tend to make life complex. This is an indulgent luxury based on our own fears. Better to go into action, and learn from those things which did not turn out the way we expected. This is where the true honour, dignity, integrity and self-worth of being an exceptional leader actually develops.

It is possible to do everything right in life and still be unsuccessful. It is also possible to do everything wrong and still have a rich life. It just depends on how we measure our success, and whose approval we are seeking. As team leaders, we can determine our success by our ability to have the approval of those who will follow us. This requires that certain steps be considered to heighten our chances of achievement. These steps include:

1. Have a clear path: go to one thing
2. Delete what is not useful: get rid of something
3. Anticipate contingencies: prepare for anything
4. Accumulate information: sort for everything

The ability to implement these steps will identify our limitations as a leader. We need to keep it simple and broad enough to encompass all possibilities. We can't stop the future, but we can shape the way it unfolds. Each of us has the qualities of a leader, yet we lack the faith in ourselves and our ability to drive and forge out a path, into something new. Not everything has to be different. We can lead people down the same path, but in a different way; ensuring they have experiences which they can enjoy, again and again.

As leaders, our goal is to teach others to lead because as they follow our example they model successful strategies along the way. People have extended themselves and overcome insurmountable odds because they believed in someone else's conviction. To lead is to command not only ourselves but those around us to achieve something of importance. Command is broken into two distinct areas: the ability to have authority over a set of circumstances, and the responsibility to ensure that the actions taken maximise successful completion of the team's endeavour. Authority incorporates the personal qualities which will allow others to follow us more easily. Responsibility will include those factors which can sometimes to be a burden to those who lead, since "The 'but' stops here." When we lead, all the excuses and failures ultimately rest on our shoulders.

It is the combination of how we demonstrate our authority and the way we take responsibility which determines our leadership style. It will be our style in leading which will enable others to unleash their individual potential while at the same time enjoy being part of a team which has purpose and direction.

Authority	**Responsible for**
Decisiveness	Success/failure
Competent	Costs
Honourable	Equipment
Dutiful	Learning
Objective	Experiences
Approachable	Welfare
Dependable	Safety

AUTHORITY

Authority is being in charge and exerting an influence on the team's proceedings. People want answers and decisions. Failing this, they want reassurance and confirmation. Approval, however, is a two-way process. That is, as leaders, we have to prove our credentials in a way that other people approve of. Team members want to see that the leader is committed to a course of action, that the strategies implemented are sound, and that the leader has the ability to be flexible in operational tactics to achieve the team's objectives. People need to see leaders who are solid in their beliefs, and strong enough to adapt and adopt new tactics to deal with the unknown, the unpredictable and the uncertainties that occur during the implementation of a project. They do not want to see leaders who are afraid of stepping forward and who allow their doubts to hold them back so that they remain contained and safe. People respect honour, dignity and integrity. These are qualities of substance that help us face the unpredictability of the future.

RESPONSIBILITY

The exceptional leader has the ability to improvise and take the initiative. It is not enough to just achieve the team's outcome, how the outcome is achieved and the learning that can be extracted during the project's implementation are equally important. In other words, the people under our command should have the opportunity to grow and develop. When we take responsibility for our actions we become more committed and determined to guarantee the team's success. It is this conviction which adds substance to the work we do. Sacrifices, compromises and giving up other things are all part of the hidden costs of being a leader. Objections, judgements and resistance are obstacles which we can use to inspire us, so that we dig deeper or shift our tactics to encompass unforeseen difficulties. An exceptional leader is able to turn a disadvantage into an advantage. Keeping in touch with our primary responsibility and steadfastly working towards the project's completion ensures a reliable progress and unwavering course of action.

STYLE

Leadership style is how we go about implementing our tactics to ensure success. Our personal delivery is what others relate to first when they follow our command. Often leadership style can cover up incompetence, where individuals seek to please and appease team members in their need for approval. These individuals do not keep their command for long. Such tactics are easily transparent. Most of us want to not only get the job done but complete the project in a way that is effective and efficient.

One style is not necessarily better than any other, since individuals require different approaches to motivate them. People will gravitate towards those styles they can respect and relate to. Each team member will have preferences and prejudices about how they wish to be managed. They will judge our leadership style by the impact we create. As authority figures, we embody all previous leaders that our staff have experienced. While we need to acknowledge these factors, we also need to set our sights firmly on the final outcome, and not waver from this objective.

Leadership style is one of our resources. People judge us by it and endeavour to predict our responses. There will be times when individuals will require being managed in a way that is not to their liking. When this occurs, we need to be aware of what responses our style can create for others. Most appreciate the difference between a leader who can be tough and fair, as opposed to being tough and mean. People respond best to balance. Whatever our personal preference in leadership style, it is also advisable to be flexible. As long as people know that our style can fluctuate, and perceive these differences every now and again, then we remain dynamic, flexible and open. We need to know when to be more, when to be less, when to lighten up, when to hold on tenaciously. When we deliver contrasts in our style, such as authoritarian, democratic, laissez faire or dictatorial, we remain unpredictable. It is important to have the ability to utilise all these styles while understanding the different impact they will have on those around us. We can then better determine which style will be the most effective, given a particular situation.

Each of us has a personal history which has shaped and moulded who we are today. It provides us with a set of resources which is the foundation for our ability to be confident and competent. Our early life was a series of challenges and tests. We learned and developed our preferred style from each of these events. The learning that we incorporate will influence the way we will respond in certain circumstances. When faced with a new challenge we generally select a response which previous experience has taught us will be the best way to respond. Inadvertently, we can build a trap for ourselves, such as "I'm not creative," or "I'm not that way, this is who I am." We become limited and predictable. Therefore we need to keep a personal history of our own style and those around us so we can assist ourselves and others to develop new skills and resources. We can begin by identifying our preferred style and the amount of time that we spend delivering this approach to our employees. Please place a mark on each continuum to indicate your preferred style:

Style

1. *Approachable*

Friendly ←→ Unfriendly
Open ←→ Closed
Carefree ←→ Cautious
Polite ←→ Discourteous
Interested ←→ Bored

2. *Communication Patterns*

Active ←→ Passive
Quiet ←→ Loud
Involved ←→ Uninvolved
Clear ←→ Vague
Simple ←→ Complex

3. *Natural Qualities*

Curious ←→ Uninterested
Creative ←→ Conservative
Intuitive ←→ Procedural
Resourceful ←→ Stuck
Tenacious ←→ Gives in

These categories are by no means complete. They are more a guideline to assist us in having a greater understanding of our own style and of our other team members. We utilise these styles as a way to manage our world and the people we influence. Everyone of course is unique and at times will produce different combinations from the previous list, depending on the situation. We can also use this list to predict how others are likely to react in the future. This will enable us to set up new challenges for their own personal development. For instance, if for 60 percent of the time an individual responds in a pessimistic way to new dilemmas, we can take the opportunity to assist this person to look at the situation from another perspective, so that their outlook is not so bleak.

Generally, we are not fully aware of how our leadership style impacts upon others since the way we respond will be affected by our emotional state at the time. We rarely stand back and analyse our reactions from an objective point of view but are often wrapped up in our own feelings. Our emotions are one of our most underrated resources because they have the capacity to instigate powerful and influential effects in others while also creating substantial damage in our relationships with team members if not properly harnessed. As managers, we need to be aware of our emotional state when making decisions, since strong emotional responses can colour objective or rational analysis.

All emotions are useful, depending on the context. For instance, we can use our anger to fire ourselves up into taking action, while enthusiasm is fundamental when selling a product or idea, and consideration essential when providing service to our customers and support to our colleagues. Similarly, passion and determination are powerful in motivating people. These emotions don't have to be used all the time, but can be selectively chosen by any leader wanting to become more expedient and effective in creating action and commitment to the team's objectives.

Leadership style is not a static event. Just as business is continually changing, we too can begin to work on our future style by adding useful personal qualities and enhancing our own natural ability. True elegance comes when we make these changes part of our natural repertoire. Initially when we incorporate new behaviours into our leadership style it won't feel comfortable and natural. It won't feel like 'us'. This feeling should be welcomed because it indicates that we are doing something different.

Fortunately, the more we utilise any new approach in the way we lead, the more it will come to feel as if we had always been this way. As leaders, we need to work out what we should use less of in our behavioural responses, since it is possible that aspects of our style may alienate or disempower team members. We can also consider what we need to use more fully to become more competent and effective when managing others. Above all, we have to create an experience of substance which people can relate to so that they too can learn how to manage us and the commands we deliver.

Chapter 5

Team Management

As team managers, we have the ability to present information in a variety of ways. We therefore can influence how someone decides what is useful and which ideas have merit. One of our primary roles is to assist another in being convinced about the direction we have chosen, so that the project becomes important to all members of the team. For most people, there are so many choices; so many things to do and so many decisions to be made.

How we use this influence will determine how we are perceived by our employees. If used wisely, we can create integrity and friendships with the people around us. If done poorly, doubt and caution will grow, not only for our project, but also for our ability to manage the team. Even projects or ideas which offer something that is extremely useful can be tainted by a poor and unprofessional delivery. For instance, in a recent survey in America, car and insurance sales people were rated the lowest by their customers as a trustworthy and credible profession. So, many honourable sales people today carry with them the legacy of past unethical practices by their colleagues.

It is not the product or service that is in question. Instead it is the people who deliver, and how they go about their work that determines trust. We have a responsibility, whichever profession we have chosen, to demonstrate a professional and ethical delivery. We do this by creating an atmosphere within the team which allows our colleagues to present the highest possible standard, and our customers to feel satisfied with the team's efforts.

PATTERNS OF INFLUENCE

Patterns of influence are inherent in every conversation we have. We are influencing at every moment, with every word that we use. We can't not influence! Excellent managers are aware of this, and select their words and messages with precision and care. Below is a list of patterns of influence which will add to the experiences we create for our team. These patterns will create in staff a sense of integrity and trust towards our project, and more importantly, towards us.

Inclusion and Exclusion

This is a subtle pattern of influence inherent in any team or group of people working together. A sense of belonging is one of our most fundamental motivators. It feels uncomfortable, and even painful, to be excluded. Most of us can remember that feeling when we were 'left out' in the playground at school. That feeling doesn't change much in adults. So, we will go to extraordinary lengths to be included.

Teams, and the projects we are implementing, need to promote a sense of belonging. When we feel that we have a place where we belong we will go to considerable effort to contribute more than our share. It becomes a privilege to be a member, and we will not jeopardise our position. We want to support our relationships and do what we can. Team leaders can utilise this pattern of influence by highlighting the benefits of belonging to the group and emphasising that everyone is an important component in the larger scheme of things; that we all add to the success of the company.

'Outsiders' want to be part of something that is special. So team managers need to not only create specialness about the project or the company but also establish the uniqueness of the ongoing work that the project requires. Simple things, such as referring to people by their name, or acknowledging an individual's efforts, particularly in front of the team, promote that sense of belonging.

Attraction

We are attracted to things which we like. We are distracted by things which are different or unusual. As team managers we can emphasise those things which our team members like, to keep them on track, and reduce the distractions. Most team members will be attracted to projects which they consider to be important and purposeful. They want to be part of a project that is special and worth doing. Therefore, team managers also need to highlight the learning which will occur for all involved for the duration of the project, together with the possibilities that this project will bring.

Service providers also operate on this principle of welcoming a customer into the 'elite', by providing that special table at the restaurant, valet parking or priority luggage check-in. This promotes a sense of specialness to customers, so they will continue to come back. It's not "what you know, but who you know", that makes us feel important!

Take an interest in your team members to find out what hopes and dreams they have. It is always attractive when others take the time to be interested in what is important to us. People will do amazing things, and believe that any difficulty is surmountable. In many cases, we can even create dreams for our team members. Think about what is attracting people to be part of the team. Find out what is important to these individuals so that they can obtain more of what they want. They are then continually motivated to produce and perform.

Purposeful distractions can be deliberately used to manage an individual's energy. When we work hard we like to have a break. Chat about anything. Notice what distracts someone away from their work, particularly if the individual has become stuck. Give time out from the hard work to those who work diligently. This reduces seriousness, and work becomes more light-hearted. Even if it means having to close off from the external world, we can always turn off the phones. When people are out of balance they don't perform consistently over time. Pressure from one task must be counteracted with more pleasurable activities in other areas.

Availability

Anything that is limited in supply is high in demand. It increases in worth and value. The scarcer something becomes, the harder it is to obtain. Its value will increase. For instance, antiques are old things that increase in worth. Similarly, land is something we cannot make, so its demand and value is increasing as the population increases. Within our teams, not all of us can be leaders, so position and status are perceived as important and valuable.

Rich experiences are the intangible ingredients that we all need in order to have meaning in our lives. Companies which provide the best service and products which are useful will be sought out. Managers and service providers who can do the same with their working strategies will have people seek them out. People will want to be part of their team. Given places on the team are limited, and so availability restricted, individuals will be motivated to be selected for the team if they see the project as a rare opportunity to make exceptional gains and if they see the team manager as someone with special qualities and skills they can learn from.

People don't value something for nothing. Managers need to point out how they can achieve, acknowledging the costs and benefits. Hard work and perseverance are tried and true methods for reaching the team's objectives while knowledge, information and skills make success more likely.

These patterns require management to go beyond just project completion, and begin to think of how they can influence team members so that they are involved and feel part of something special. Relationships need to be ongoing, rather than a 'once-off' transaction. Otherwise people move on, probably to our competitors! We have missed the mark.

If we wish to maintain a substantial share in the business world, we need to remain focused on the team members' needs; both for today and tomorrow. While we can create and generate the needs of others, we must also deliver projects that provide personal satisfaction and appeal. These processes are simple to implement, but only if the team manager views the world from the employees' point of view. Making that little bit extra effort in understanding another builds an attraction to our project, our team and us! For most of us, it's the little things in life, together with the simple gestures that make our decisions easy. As managers of a team, it is our job to continually strive and promote the personal growth of our staff. Doing so will ensure these relationships will continue into the future; that they will want to return for more. And so the job of managing becomes easier, as it builds upon itself!

Facilitation

Facilitation is the process of allowing others to maximise their own ability. As team leaders we actively take part in ensuring the work environment is conducive to meeting the needs of our team members. In other words, we are building the setting and experiences which will enable people to perform. When we facilitate we assist others to produce. We can give the pointers that set the direction for others to follow. Our most important role as a manager is to keep things progressing and moving forward.

The greatest facilitators are those who connect others with their personal resources, so that these individuals learn and develop. This then allows them to take on new skills, behaviours and abilities. Facilitators focus on the team's direction, with the single purpose of making it easier for the team to function and achieve its direction. These people are prepared to go first to assist the facilitation process. They model the rules and standards of communication expected within the team. They actively demonstrate what is required by others. Areas of communication that enable others to judge the effectiveness of the team will include:

1. Giving feedback: How do you do this?
What do you say?
Was the feedback balanced?
Who should receive it?
When should it be received?
2. Receiving feedback: Can you take it?
How do you respond?
What you do with it?
3. How much time do you spend with participants, giving everyone the personal touches? Has anyone been ignored?
4. How do you relate differently/similarly with each team member?
5. When do you interrupt, and how do you do this to increase involvement by others?

6. What management style do you use to impose rules/ expectations on the group?

Consider how you would display the following attributes to team members:

Behaviour Actions required, movements, gestures, facial expressions	**Words** Lists words that affect the following:
Individual uniqueness, worth and value	
Give and take, to work together	
Acknowledging another's dreams and future potential	

One company we worked with was asked to fill in the above table. They identified that to demonstrate individual uniqueness and worth there needs to be gestures and facial expressions which are warm and approachable. When others are contributing their ideas, this needs to be acknowledged by paying attention and not dismissing their input as irrelevant. Perhaps the most expedient way of demonstrating individual worth is to ask questions, to gather team members' opinions. By asking for someone's opinion, then really listening to their answer, you are showing others that their opinions count. We can also acknowledge another's dreams and future potential, by first gaining information about what they are, then identify specifically how the current project will assist the individual move closer to their dreams.

FACILITATING TASKS

The setting of tasks for all team members sets a direction and assists the team in coming closer to their objectives and the successful completion of the project. It also produces something tangible for them to relate to. Small, attainable accomplishments build the cycle of productivity and self-worth. We need to make clear distinctions between those tasks which are of interest, and those tasks that seem to be almost daily chores. We all have chores to do, and they are just as important in achieving the final goal. The role of the facilitator is to allocate tasks in a way that will efficiently increase performance:

Leaders' task	**Members' task**
Go first, model the task	Replicate the action
Give support	Refine the action
Take risks	Add the challenge

The facilitator's role is to allocate tasks and skills, to obtain the very best from all team members. Everyone should be given the opportunity to utilise their personal resources, and also add to their repertoire of skills and knowledge; to become more competent and experienced. As facilitators for both the project leader and members of the team we have a responsibility to make sure this happens. To assist in this process, there are a range of questions which will give pointers on how to build a direction for the team:

1. What tasks are useful and important in achieving the team's objectives?
2. Who will be the most suitable to complete these tasks?
3. Where and when should these tasks be completed?
4. How can we plan for the unexpected?
5. What personal style would best suit my role as facilitator?
6. What can I learn from the feedback I received, particularly to do differently next time?

With each project that needs to be broken down into component parts and then distributed amongst team members, the facilitator should specifically ask:

- *What* is the task needed to be completed?
- *What* components parts can be distributed throughout the team?
- *Why* are we doing this?
- *Who* will be responsible for completion of each task and *why*?
- *When* will this occur?
- *Where* will this occur?
- *Who* can give additional support or backup if required?"

Team Structure

People are the most important components of good team work. Individuals working together become a powerful force which is more enduring than flashes of individual brilliance. Most individuals and their talents are under-valued, by themselves and others. In isolation, they may not have all the requirements to do all the things which are required, but together they can accomplish extraordinary things. Together, their dreams of 'What's possible?' is just the beginning.

As facilitators, we need to know the pieces that make up the whole puzzle. We therefore need to take a detailed inventory of the myriad of skills, qualities and talents that we have represented in each team member:

What has been identified? → ← **What needs to be developed?**

Skills
Knowledge
Resources
Qualities
Potential

This inventory should be completed meticulously, with attention given to detail so that nothing goes unnoticed. We can also have team members contribute, so that the list provides a description of all the resources available. This will make the facilitator's role considerably easier. It is also an opportunity to view with pride the potential that lies waiting to be realised.

DELEGATION

When we delegate we hand over responsibility. For some people delegation is an easy process, and for others it is difficult. When we delegate, we place our expectations and faith in another. People want challenges, but need to understand what this actually means. By being active in the process of delegation, it allows us time to think things through, and plan how best to act. The process of delegating can be exciting, in that it allows so many possibilities. Primarily it can:

- Involve people and co-operation
- Build challenges and achievements
- Set a direction for others
- Promote ownership and commitment
- Give feedback about others' ability and potential
- Incorporate other styles and perspectives
- Free up our time and energy for other things
- Fully utilise resources

However the intentions behind delegating can often be misunderstood, particularly if the personal style of the team leader is not respected. Some of the drawbacks on delegating include:

- Can be perceived as off-loading work
- It may take longer in the short term
- The job may not be done exactly to our specifications
- Being accountable and taking a risk in another's work

With an ever increasing workload and demand for quality, we have to hand over some of the responsibilities, ensuring that the job gets done. Delegation is a testament to our knowledge and faith in people, and the ability to communicate what is required. When we delegate tasks and responsibilities, we need to consider:

1. What to delegate?
   - If I do this, what benefits, both in the short and long term, does this have for the project?
   - If I don't do this what else could I do, both in the short and long term?
   - What does this do for our development and growth, both now and in the future?
2. Who to delegate?
   - What abilities and attributes are necessary for those doing the job?
   - Which person(s) has these abilities and attributes?
   - What do they need to achieve what's required?
   - What long-term benefits exist for these individuals?
3. When and how to delegate?
   - When would be the best time to delegate?
   - How to approach the person?
   - How to motivate, then set the direction?
   - How to maintain, support and guide these individuals?
   - How to reward, and make individuals accountable?

Delegating Steps

Delegating is a process to assist us in ensuring that what we want, in terms of a successful project, actually occurs. The project needs to have steps which break down the enormity of the task into functional and workable parts. Each outcome builds upon itself, to achieve the direction and expected result.

When we divide the tasks into manageable components, it becomes easier to overcome the concerns and difficulties. A step-by-step approach allows us to experience a sense of progression, as we move closer to our destination:

1. *Vision*

   Project an image, and paint the challenge, "What if?" Go for the overall picture or idea. Let it be expansive.

2. *Valuing*

   Attend to objections, and limiting beliefs. Notice individuals' likes and dislikes. This will identify the processes that may interfere with the purpose of the team.

3. *Detailing*

   Move into details. What can be done to avoid the obstacles? Begin the process of directing.

4. *Tasking*

   Marry the team members' skills and resources with the tasks that need to be completed. These connections will allow the process of delegation to run more smoothly.

5. *Adaptation*

   Connecting individual tasks into pairs, triads, groups, and forming special projects teams.

6. *Formation*

   Maintenance, and updating targets and expectations. Connecting outcomes to form a vision for a new beginning.

TRACKING

There is so much to keep track of when orchestrating a team. We track to gather all the relevant information, prioritise and construct what needs to be implemented, and read the signals that people give as they interact with other team members. This requires experience, or the ability to learn, and to remain open to possibilities. At all times, the team leader needs to watch for responses that team members demonstrate for these will be crucial in determining the project's success.

A leader's tracking of the team can be clouded in many ways. The surest way is to test the ground in front of us, take nothing for granted and assume only that we will learn. The following processes are ways to help us keep track of all that is going on around us:

Back Track

This is the ability to know where we have gone. If the team leader finds that the team is heading down a blind alley, then we can back track, that is, go back to where the team started. We can reiterate information and reinforce strategies that have been successful in the past. We can check on what learning has been extracted, particularly with the mistakes that have been made. The team leader can ask a number of questions to facilitate the process of back tracking:

- Where did we start from?
- What did we do along the way?
- How did we prioritise the tasks that need to be completed?
- What were the highlights for the team?
- What were the areas which we still need to explore?

For learning to be more established we need to cover old ground more than once, so that it becomes familiar and more solid for team members. Three to five times is minimum for most people. Very few people will have 'one-take' learning. Those that do usually have an interest or passion, although they may become impatient in the group since they learn faster.

Future Track

The team leader can also take the learning which has been gained into the future. Team members can be guided on how to apply this new knowledge in future teams and projects. Information gained will only remain relevant if it is seen as useful, and used more fully. Team members require practical applications both for the future, and in different situations, if these individuals are to personally grow from the experiences they have received as being part of our team. To facilitate this process we can ask a number of questions which will identify future applications:

- Where is this learning going to be useful?
- Who will it involve?
- How can we extract more learning from this information?
- When is this to be used?
- How long will it be for?
- How often can this information be used?

This is important in ensuring that learning for team members remains current and used in the future, rather than being stored as past memories. We are building these individuals a map of a new territory, which they need to explore. Offer them some guidance and reassurance that they are on the right track.

Sidetrack

While the team leader needs to be aware of the amount of time team members are becoming sidetracked, it is not automatically a non-productive activity for the team. At times, team members will benefit from being sidetracked from the project's objectives. This is useful when individuals need to have breathing space from something that is difficult, or to give them the space to offer their opinion. These responses are an insight into how they associate, generalise and create new learning. Their perspectives will always be useful since they are an integral part of the team process.

Often another view will introduce new concepts which other team members had failed to notice. This builds possibilities and can broaden our horizons. Becoming sidetracked can also make connections that are relevant between the current project and future applications, or new connections between the current project and other situations in the company.

Fast and Slow Track

During the progress of the team's project there will be times to challenge individuals' normal rate of learning and personal change. When we fast-track information individuals quickly get into doing the tasks or procedures so that they learn through practical experience. Little time is spent on ensuring that they understand the meaning behind the activity. Just doing becomes more important. This also gives the team member useful learning in that they appreciate it is possible to complete an action without thoroughly understanding every facet of the procedure.

Alternatively, slow track is useful for team members to comprehend and gain understanding of the tasks required. Sometimes we need people to think for themselves, rather than follow directions. This builds initiative and allows them to make sense of their experience. Slow track is allowing individuals to go at a pace which is comfortable for them, particularly when the procedures are complex, understanding is important and when mistakes will be costly to the successful completion of the project.

Multi Track

Multi track is what most effective managers will be doing for the majority of their working day. To become more expedient, it is useful for team members to do more than one thing at a time. Most people learn sequentially, piece by piece, step-by-step. Yet they also need to assimilate information. When this occurs, learning will become a habit. We are then able to do more than one thing at a time. Knowing where all the pieces fit and what can be done simultaneously makes learning more powerful. The team can then build clusters of operations when routines become established, familiar and thoroughly understood.

Chapter 6

Rapport: Connecting with Others

Recognition, respect and reassurance are valued by us all. We all want a place where we feel important, a place where we feel at home. When we give recognition, respect and reassurance to others they feel more at home with us, and when we receive it from others, we are more likely to stay. The team becomes more cohesive, difficulties can be overcome more tenaciously, and performance improves.

Recognition is noticing the differences in others. It is being attentive, making judgments, and acknowledging someone else is important. Recognition allows us to observe the differences and appreciate what is unique about these patterns of behaviour. We can then compare how another perceives the world differently from us. It may be that they have some useful strategies that we wish to include as our own.

Respect is understanding that there is a difference in how people behave, and what they consider relevant. It's easier to respect another's beliefs and behaviours when they are similar to our own. It is more difficult to respect those patterns that are different from our own because they directly challenge our model of the world. We have to compare these differences with the way we respond, and at times this can make us feel uncomfortable. When we respect another we appreciate the differences that they bring to the team, rather than endeavour to make these individuals more like us.

Reassurance is accepting and being considerate to the differences that we have noticed. By reassuring members on our team, we send the message that mistakes are a learning opportunity, and that their behaviours are not a matter of being good or bad; some are just more productive than others. We all want reassurance, particularly when the going gets tough, when we are doing something new or taking a risk, and when we feel uncertain about our own abilities and contribution to the team.

Respecting our own strengths and weaknesses allows us the opportunity to draw on others, that is, be helpful and respectful to others, and notice what is useful. All of us face uncertainty and will require reassurance. If things are not working ask three questions:

1. What am I not recognising?
2. What have I failed to respect?
3. How else can I reassure?

When we notice those things that are different in others, it actually allows us to connect with those things which are the same. This gives a reassurance to team members of a shared reality, while respecting those things which make us unique. All of us want to be recognised for who we are and also for our potential. We can also offer strategies to assist others and reassure them as they face their own difficulties.

Being 'response-able' allows us to be responsible for our actions within a relationship. Becoming aware of how to recognise, respect and reassure all possible responses builds the ability to have more dynamic and productive relationships. These relationships will need to incorporate diverse values and beliefs of other members of the team. Acknowledge what is different, rather than demand things be done our way. This allows us to get on with business, and to work together on the important issues, instead of being side tracked by irrelevant distractions. This is important in negotiating all relationships, from family issues and team building to global politics.

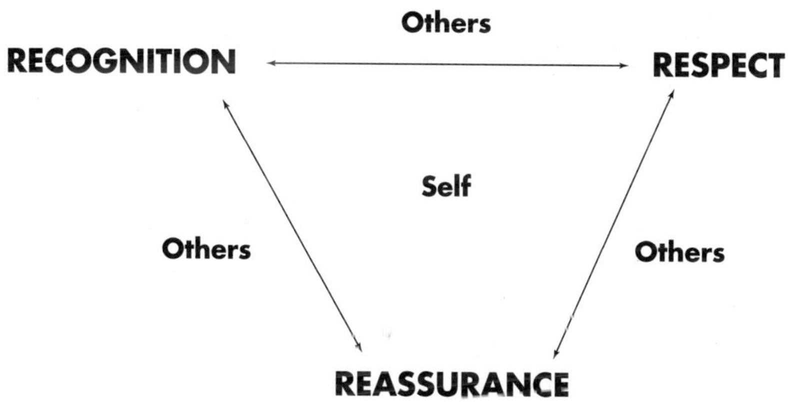

BEING IN RAPPORT WITH OURSELVES

The most important relationship we will ever have is the one we have with ourselves. What really matters to us? What is the substance that counts? To have rapport internally is to explore our criteria for what matters to us, and to have an understanding of our beliefs and values.

Before we can influence others, we must first influence ourselves. Knowing ourselves is about acknowledging and accepting who we are and the variety of abilities and skills we bring to the team. We do this by giving ourselves recognition, respect and reassurance:

Recognition

- What physical features do you recognise as unique in you?
- What skills and qualities do you recognise in yourself?
- What beliefs do you have that may be limiting?

Respect

- What is important to you?
- How are you different from others?
- What beliefs do you have that enhance you?

Reassurance

- How are you thoughtful and considerate to yourself?
- How do you acknowledge the learning that you gain from your mistakes?
- How do you care for yourself, when you have fears or concerns?

We need to identify and build a sense of balance between how we recognise, respect and reassure ourselves. In relating to someone else, we have to be aware of our strengths and weaknesses. More importantly, we need to be aware of our biases and the value judgments that we have about others.

If our weakest area is in recognition of ourselves, we tend to be unable to discern between our emotions, and be insensitive to our own needs. We can also be inattentive to others, and not be aware that our behaviour affects those around us.

If respect to ourselves is our weakest area, we may be unable to appreciate all our qualities, and so don't display all the facets that make up who we are. These people can become easily frustrated, often putting themselves down in private. Publicly however, they wish to remain in control, so that they are less likely to display vulnerability to others.

If reassurance to ourselves is the weakest area, we tend not to look after ourselves. We can be too hard when evaluating our performance within the team. These people may find it difficult to receive compliments, and may take feedback negatively, by generalising and amplifying the feedback to describe all of themselves, when in reality, it was only directed to a specific context.

BEING IN RAPPORT WITH OTHERS

When we think of the relationships we have, they will vary in the degree of rapport we have with the people concerned. For instance, we treat our close friends differently from acquaintances and those individuals whom we have difficulty with. The differences will be in how we give them recognition, respect and reassurance. Explore now these differences which exist between these different relationships:

Showing recognition to:	Good friend
	Acquaintance
	Strained relationship
Showing respect to:	Good friend
	Acquaintance
	Strained relationship
Showing reassurance to:	Good friend
	Acquaintance
	Strained relationship

When we examine our relationships we can learn about how we treat these people differently. We can also ascertain which is our strongest and weakest areas. Once again, most of us will have an area which will dominate, and an area where we do the least work in how we give recognition, respect and reassurance to another.

Not recognising another may mean we miss the changes that they are going through. We may not notice all their qualities and abilities and be insensitive to their needs. Instead, we may see them as stereotypes, rather than acknowledge the variety of roles they perform, and the diverse responsibilities that they must meet.

Not respecting someone else can mean that they feel unheard, that their views are not considered, and that they feel of little value when they are with us. People have different beliefs and values, which in turn produce different behaviours. We may not like these behaviours or understand them, but it is still possible to acknowledge the differences that exist.

Not reassuring another may not allow them to save face, particularly when they have made a mistake. We are unable to give the support or back-up when they need it the most. Often they feel taken for granted, because they receive no feedback that their contribution is important. This can lead to feelings of being exposed and vulnerable, which perpetuates poor self-worth and low self-esteem.

Exercise

Explore how you give recognition, respect and reassurance to enhance your relationships:

1. Select 2 people that you feel lukewarm about. Create an image of these two people.
2. Build up this image of person 1, by seeing him/her with respect, reassurance and recognition.
3. Also build up the image of person 2, by seeing him/her with disrespect, non-reassurance and doubt.
4. Look at the differences between the two. How do you feel towards these 2 individuals? (Remember, the choice is yours when seeing another!)

Our teams, of course, are made up of individuals. They are our strongest asset. We know they are more than working machines, but require recognition, respect and reassurance. We need to take a good look at the internal structure of our team. When things are not working, it may be that those working for us are not having their needs met:

Recognition

- How do you recognise your team's potential?
- How do you recognise success and achievements?
- How do you recognise the ambitions of those working for you?
- How do you recognise any difficulties that your team members may be experiencing?

Respect

- How do you respect the individual, so that they are more than just part of the team?
- How do you give equal value to the many different jobs and functions that your team members perform?
- How do you acknowledge individual differences, especially when someone takes a risk, and does it differently?

Reassurance

- How do you give reassurance that we are all going in the same direction, even though we have different roles to perform?
- How do you give reassurance that this team delivers a sense of loyalty and trust?
- How do you give reassurance that mistakes are a way of learning, and exploring new challenges?
- How do you give reassurance that difficulties can be overcome with supervision and training?
- How do you give reassurance that opportunities are available to those who wish to grow?

Employees, at all levels of the company, are the heartbeat of doing business. While it is essential to be prospecting new customers and maintaining their needs, the business will not last long if the internal company structure is fragmented. Team members will only stay if their needs are being met. This applies through all levels of the company, from senior executives to the cleaners. None should be forgotten!

Keeping Good Company

There are however different rules, mostly unspoken, that impose a structure which allows for more workable relationships. We all have beliefs about authority. We learned these beliefs from our family. It was established very early on who set the rules in the home, and what happened if these rules weren't obeyed. We were taught what loyalty means, and how to treat our elders or people in authority, such as our teachers. These rules were seldom discussed in detail.

For most of us, we carry these rules with us into the workplace. While we all require recognition, respect and reassurance in our dealing with others, the higher a person goes up the corporate ladder, the more respect is usually observed. Senior executives and team leaders are responsible for direction and leadership. They require respect to do their job well so that others will follow. These individuals need to be self-motivated and self-directed and be able to make decisions about a project's direction without requiring reassurance from other levels of the company.

However, the role of the members of the team is to follow directives and commit themselves to the objectives that have been set out. Therefore, they require reassurance that their performance is on track, and that following directives will allow the project to achieve its goals. While recognition is something we all require, middle management constantly monitor and anticipate the needs of both senior executives and of individuals within the team.

Senior Executives	(More Respect)
Middle Management	(More Recognition)
Team Members	(More Reassurance)

Respect

The amount of respect we give another demonstrates their position in the company. Invariably, the more senior the position in the organisation, the more respect these individuals are shown. Team members need to acknowledge and follow the structure that has been put in place. It is mostly appropriate for employees to seek assistance or clarification at the next senior level to themselves. This has been designed to maximise executive functioning. We can show respect in the following ways:

- Allow that person more space; we tend to stand back.
- Address them more formally; virtually no use of nicknames.
- Listen when they are talking; we tend not to interrupt.
- Polite behaviour, normally reserved for acquaintances.

Reassurance

People at the top make the tough decisions. It is the people at the 'bottom', however, who implement them. The most important point with all projects and new ideas is to give reassurance to those directly involved. This will have these changes activated faster and more efficiently. Reassurance can be shown in the following ways:

- Warm expressions of support and congratulations at a job well done.
- An explanation of the benefits of the changes being implemented.
- A genuine openness to any difficulties or excuses that might arise.
- Down-to-earth, clear guidelines on the procedures to be followed.

All too often, however, little reassurance is given to the workers and team players who are the ones who give the organisation its substance. Even the most brilliant company policy or guideline becomes irrelevant if there is no one to implement it, and play the game!

Recognition

All employees want a sense of value and worth within the company. We all need to feel important, that our contribution makes a difference and that our work has value. Companies grow like families when they work together as teams. It is the job of middle management to implement changes, to make recommendations and create order. Each area, and more importantly, the people who work in these areas, need to be recognised as an integral part of the successful system. Support can be given to all employees, by showing recognition in the following ways:

- Acknowledge their skills and the effort taken to get the job completed.
- Ask their opinions or feedback about how things could be done differently.
- Gather information about their moods; notice whether they are tense or relaxed.
- People are more than workers or executives. Know their interests outside work.

All relationships within the organisation are maintained by distance. This space will indicate very quickly where the two individuals are in the company hierarchy. As with our customers, senior executives and team leaders need to connect quickly with their front-line staff, so that they can leave a lasting impression after they have gone.

We can also take a look at what our team does, as a whole, to show recognition, respect and reassurance to the company, to demonstrate to others the value of the team:

Recognition

- How do you recognise business opportunities when they occur?
- How do you recognise trends in the market place?
- How do you recognise the business done by your competitors?
- How do you recognise customer demands?
- What excuses does your team give you when things go wrong?

Respect

- How do you test your product in the market place?
- How do you place value or importance in product development?
- How does your company deliver what it says it does?
- How does it maintain an ongoing relationship with customers?
- How do you ask for feedback, rather than wait to receive it?
- What do you do with the feedback, once you have received it?
- How quickly do you respond to criticism that you receive?

Reassurance

- How do you give value for money?
- How do you ensure that you provide a quality product?
- How do you give reassurance in the ongoing service you provide?
- How do your customers know you are committed to meeting their needs?
- What quality control and guarantees do you give your customers?

Getting into rapport with others requires that we give them recognition, respect and reassurance. It means that we must go beyond ourselves, notice what is going on around us and relate to other people, objects and events.

THE PERSONAL TOUCHES

We all crave the personal touches because it lets us know that we are not being taken for granted. For this reason, personal touches will always make an impact. They are the little things that virtually take no time and cost the company nothing. But they can increase quality of work and enhance loyalty. They can range from hearing our name, a friendly gesture, or a warm smile. Ross Pierot takes the time to know the names of all his 10,000 employees, and to be personable when meeting them. No doubt they get a buzz when the 'big boss' calls them by name as he walks through the factory.

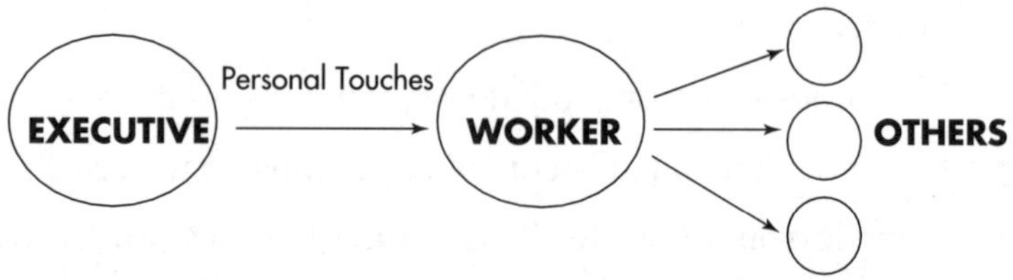

These personal touches narrow the gap that the pecking order has created. The team leader moves into the employee's personal space, creates an impact, and leaves an impression that lingers. This impression will be passed onto others.

Even if we are unable to move closer to all our employees, making the attempt with a handful of staff sets up the generalisation that we are people of integrity who care. This gets passed along at coffee breaks and in the canteen. As leaders, we are creating our own image within the company, as well as with our public, business associates and customers.

Rapport is the fabric which binds teams together. The personal touches will allow individuals to connect with all team members by showing recognition, respect and reassurance. Each day we need to create a high profile by delivering personal touches to those around us.

Of course, the personal touches go both ways. Kindness is repaid in kind. The chief executive of a large wholesaler in Melbourne was known for his personal touches. He not only knew the names of all his employees, he also knew into how things were going at home for his workers. He supported those families who were experiencing difficulties in the most generous of ways, because family life was all important. Workers were given Christmas bonuses at a time when they were almost unheard of. When the union arrived and insisted that the company join, the workers jeered and made it known that the union couldn't offer anything more than what they already getting from Mr Leo! He was loved by all who worked for him. Staff turnover and sick leave was incredibly low. One employee had actually worked for the firm for 50 years! Loyalty and commitment, once given, becomes a two-way street.

Now when Mr Leo reached old age, he still came into work early every morning without fail to assist the drivers in reversing their vans out of the huge garage. There he would be in a three-piece suit, signalling to the driver that everything was clear. The driver of course was experienced, but still young enough to be Mr Leo's grandson. No one let on that his assistance was not needed, because this was a tradition that was treasured. It allowed Mr Leo to feel that he was still an important part of what he and his wife had created. When he died all the shops in the area closed, and the people lined the streets as the funeral procession went by.

In the business world, he had been extremely successful – by being thorough, not tough. He is still remembered, because he was a man of absolute integrity. His impact lives on, and he could still teach many top executives today about how to leave an impact that will create a working environment where staff want to come each day and do their best; it's about keeping good company!

7 Days to Powerful Teams

Delivering a Sense of Unity

DAY 1: A SENSE OF YEARNING
The notion of going beyond

Each of us strive for the things we like and want from ourselves, our relationships and our lives. There are many opportunities to choose from, and each of us select a few. These yearnings become the basis of all projects, fuelled by the belief that something is attainable and worth the commitment. Teams are founded by a collection of spirits, striving to achieve the same end or common goal. Family and sports are where we probably have our first encounter of becoming a member of a team, where people work together, relying on each to do their part, and sharing in the success or failure.

What makes a group of people want the same things? Is it because we can't achieve what we want on our own? Perhaps we draw courage from others to overcome our doubts, or that someone has a vision which is alluring to us; like moths to a flame. Throughout the ages, in any endeavour, we have learned that groups of people, such as families, crews or patrols, can achieve more. In addition, it is the experiences and relationships that generate from teamwork that makes all the effort worthwhile. Companionship and a common goal cements and bonds people together.

What do we yearn for? It is either those things we want to recapture from the past, have more of in the present or the new things that we only dream of. We yearn for more of what we like, and less of what we don't like. Today corporations spend millions of dollars on marketing, creating a need for things we haven't even considered. These companies know how to create a desire. Concepts such as beauty, youth, sex appeal, power, wealth and intelligence have been used again and again in association with particular products. But even these have trends. As cultures develop we are moving more towards environmental, ecological, health and compassionate needs which we must face in the future.

Ironically, it is irrelevant what we yearn for. The important thing is that we strive forward, to complete or add something to our lives and the lives of those who are important to us. As managers with projects that need to be completed, not only do we have to capture the attention of the people involved, we also have to make the end point, or successful completion, compelling for all concerned.

Often people will get lost or sidetracked along the way. Therefore we need to break the project, as with any experience, down into a simple structure which individuals can understand. For instance, team members need to appreciate that every project has a beginning, middle and ending. By doing this we can allow people to remain focused upon the project, and direct them to continue onwards.

Structures of a Project Cycle

All experiences have a beginning, middle and ending. This structure is simple to follow and allows us to keep track of our people and their experiences, and the progress made. This structure allows us to take any experience, such as loyalty or trust, and examine which emotions and beliefs have to be there at the beginning, middle and end of the experience.

Beginning

At the beginning of an experience there will be emotions and beliefs that will limit our progress, and those that will enhance performance. In the past, or when facing change, large amounts of money and energy were expended in motivating employees. Knowing the structure of an experience allows us to build the experience, save our time and money, and have people become self-motivated. If we deliver something which is plausible, in an enthusiastic way, people will come towards it.

Middle

There will also be emotions and beliefs in the middle of an experience that will enhance our progress, and those that will limit us from moving on. When people become stuck or uncertain, don't rescue them and rob them of the experience. Encourage people to find their own solutions. This is a time of ironing out the operational difficulties and refining what works well. Involve employees rather than take over; otherwise they don't evolve. When we see frustration, we can give them another piece of information so they can continue towards the project's completion.

Ending

We need to direct employees to a point where they can appreciate the progress that has occurred, and ensure that they celebrate these gains. For each ending is only a part of the larger experience of life. Therefore, it is better to build many achievements that ultimately encourage people onto the next experience with enthusiasm and curiosity. We can deal with the sense of loss and move on to other experiences by extracting the useful learning which can be applied in the future. In doing so, we develop hindsight by taking people back through the process. We can also illustrate how their emotions affected their attitude and performance.

PARAMETERS OF YEARNING: EMOTIONS AND BELIEFS

Beliefs and emotional reactions can increase work productivity and job satisfaction, however they can also quickly dismantle a team, stop the production line and sabotage the very best management decisions. Emotional reactions are also likely to be heightened during a time of company change, as people become concerned about their own security and job predictability. As managers, knowing where we are in the experience, and where someone else is in their experience, greatly assists us in the probability of success.

Emotions which are likely to occur as the project progresses include:

Beginning ***Motivation***	**Middle** ***Management***	**Ending** ***Celebration***
Emotions that limit us from continuing	Emotions that limit us from our potential:	Emotions that limit us from a new beginning:
Doubt/concern Anxiety Apprehension Scepticism Fear Intrepidation	Uncertainty Boredom Irritation Loss Stuck Fatigue	Disappointment Disillusionment Loss Sadness Failure Regret
↓	↓	↓
To reduce, be convincing	**Acknowledge the progress and clarity**	**Celebrate the learning**

Beginning ***Motivation***	**Middle** ***Management***	**Ending** ***Celebration***
Emotions that enhance going forward:	Emotions that enhance continuing forward:	Emotions that enhance doing the experience again:
Anticipation Excitement Exhilaration Curiosity/Intrigue Interest Desire Wonder	Enthusiasm Dedication Commitment Tenacity Persistence Focused Perseverance Passion	Satisfaction Achievement Fulfilment Success Relief Joy Jubilation
↓	↓	↓
Direct enthusiasm to what's plausible	**Encourage what's probable**	**Ensuring a rich experience**

There are no clear distinctions between these different processes. That is, as one thing is ending, another is beginning. For instance, anticipation will occur at the beginning of an experience. We can, however, celebrate this single experience, then link it with enthusiasm to carry on with the job. After all, it is the end of the beginning. To move forward, we can then link anticipation to enthusiasm, to carry on with the task.

Be supportive of what others are experiencing around us, for no matter what the emotion, it is real to them. Never dismiss their feelings as irrelevant, because when we do, we are giving the message that they, as individuals, are irrelevant. Instead, create more options, so that these individuals have a greater selection of emotions from which to choose. Invariably, they will select the response that is the most useful for them. Respect their choice.

Managers are required to manage individuals' strengths. Some employees are great at the beginning of an experience. They become fired up very quickly, but tend to fade off when the job gets tough. Others are good at endings, but not necessarily good at persisting with tasks and will go for short cuts. When managing people who enjoy endings, we need to create celebrations at the beginning and middle of the experience. Similarly, for those who are good at the middle of an experience, we need to celebrate the beginning and ending.

Most of life is in the middle. There is a safety and comfort in dealing with these emotions because we stay with what we know. Each one of these builds something substantial which is important. So we manage the project and we manage the people. We build a useful experience for all involved, and target those experiences that extract the potential of individuals. As managers we also need to add and develop those beliefs that enhance performance and shift those beliefs that limit performance.

Beliefs which are likely to occur as the project progresses include:

Beginning	Middle	End
Limit (*Conservative*)	**Limit** (*Blaming*)	**Limit** (*Excuses*)
It can't be done.	It's too tough.	It wasn't worthwile.
It's not possible.	More than we expected.	We didn't make it.
We need more resources.	I haven't got the answers.	It's not good enough.
Not enough time.	We don't understand.	We couldn't work it out.
This is not right.	They have no idea.	Too much was expected.
We can't do it.	We didn't plan for this.	Don't want to be part of it.
Enhance (*Innovation*)	**Enhance** (*Involvement*)	**Enhance** (*Delivery*)
What if?	How else would we do this?	Together you did it.
What the heck!	Not much more needed.	Wasn't that easy?

continued ...

... continued from page 75

Enhance (*Innovation*)	**Enhance** (*involvement*)	**Enhance** (*Delivery*)
Let's do it.	It's getting close.	We made it happen.
This is simple/easy.	Things are going according to plan.	We got there.
If we don't someone else will.	We're getting better results than we thought.	Phew, that was close.
I want it.	What a challenge.	What a challenge.
When do we begin?	We've come so far.	Let's celebrate a job well done.
What's stopping us?	What do you need?	What did we learn from this?
How come we didn't think of it before?	We are creating something new.	What can we get from this that we haven't realised?
I can't wait to begin.		
Add 5 more:	**Add 5 more:**	**Add 5 more:**
↓	↓	↓
Enthuse	**Encourage**	**Celebrate**

As managers we need to ascertain which beliefs are useful in moving employees through an experience. Encourage those beliefs that add to the relationships at work, develop people's potential and increase performance. Acknowledge those individuals who have the openness to explore a variety of beliefs and select the one that will be the most useful for them.

Case Study

The "three musketeers" were one of the most successful teams, selling engineering parts internationally. Each of them had a natural ability and preference to do one part of the project. Bob, with his natural enthusiasm, loved the challenge of prospecting and finding new customers. But he couldn't stand the endless negotiations, meetings and detailed specifications required. This is where Ted, who knew his stuff, loved working with the intricate details. His enthusiasm and commitment to all technical aspects bought a professional quality to the team. Reg on the other hand loved the scent of a deal, with the possibility of a bargain. He was usually called upon to finalise and close the deal.

Together they worked for ten years creating a successful team and enjoying each other's company. Over the years they had great understanding of how each person was involved in the process.

When I met them in 1992 their worst fears were confirmed. They were to be disbanded as a team. They had doubts about their own performance in working on their own, since they had become probably too specialised. In reality, however, each individual had actually completed the whole process themselves. With each of their work there still has to be an end to a beginning. I asked them: For Bob, How do you know when to hand over? For Ted, how do you know when to begin negotiations and specifying? And Reg always knew what was still to be worked through before he could close.

We had to reorientate them to the specific beliefs and skills required for completion of the task. For Bob, who liked opening, we pointed out there are many openings during the course of the sale. Prospecting is an opening, but so is the beginning of negotiations, as well as the beginning of closure. For Reg, who adored the feel of closing the deal, he had to re-punctuate his experience into three closures; wrapping up of prospecting new customers, ending specific discussions, and finally, the closure of the deal. By making the whole experience more manageable and focusing them on their natural talents, they were able to see they had all the skills required to complete the job on their own. In reality, through years of friendship and discussions, each really did know a lot about how the others worked.

Two members of the team are still working for the same company, while the third has gone to set up his own business. Rather than being specialists with specialist skills, they are now specialists with generalists skills. In fact, they laughed at the simple realisation that they had the skills all along, and began the process of re-negotiating my fee for something so obvious. Well, it was a beginning. I told them that each had to do it individually!

Transcript

A sense of yearning is deeply rooted in each of us. We have always longed for something better. We have a desire to achieve something worthwhile, or to own and possess those things which we believe are valuable to us. As managers, if we don't plan for this we have to spend our time, money and energy on motivating others to do their job.

In fact, you may have noticed that motivation seems to have shifted. Perhaps management have been successful in that people are more self-motivated now. The major reason for this is telecommunications. Through the guise of entertainment, such as television, telecommunications has created a future which is compelling. We can see that now, more than at any other time in our history, we have more options and more things we can buy.

Those things which are scarce or rare become the most powerful future yearnings. Being the same is easy, so we tend to yearn for the same things. For instance, we all want a house and a car. However it is what we do with each of these which actually determines their worth.

To be accepted, acknowledged and admired are values of the twentieth century. The yearnings of tomorrow is what business will be directed towards. With work becoming a scarcity in certain parts of the world, and higher education degrees more commonplace, we have a whole new realm of yearnings which are yet to be developed. Peace and the desire to get on with others is one value which we are attempting to fulfil right now, because the cost of not accomplishing this is more devastating than at any other time in our development.

Creativity and the ability to think in a variety of ways are the commodities of the future. How we harness this potential is our challenge. We have the right ingredients. Often we become distracted by what we want to buy. These things are only the padding which brings contentment only in the moment. They are not the substance of life and do not bind people together and make life worthwhile. They just make things more comfortable and a bit easier.

We all want better relationships and different experiences. As managers, we can facilitate these yearnings, and contribute in a way more significant than we ever imagined. These abstracts, such as trust, loyalty, honour and integrity, make having all the other things worthwhile, for without these qualities we only have comfort and loneliness. People want to go beyond, partake and be involved in something. No matter how small this involvement is, at least we took part. Whether it be as individuals or as teams, we all have something to offer. Making a future where we all take part is about unleashing our potential.

Exercise of Day 1: A Sense of Yearning

Disposition

Usefulness

1. To build a desire.
2. To add momentum.
3. Prepare to move off (inertia and acceleration).

Concepts to Be Remembered

- Hunger and keenness fuel action.
- It is a long way between being gifted and being able to produce.
- All of us have a part to play. Some of us are good at beginnings (motivators), some at middles (stable workers) and others at endings (completers).
- Energy creates energy. People are drawn to it.

Steps

1. Explore the emotions and the position group members have within a project. Identify your preference. Do you prefer beginnings, middles or ends?
2. Take one area you prefer least, then work out strategies for being able to counter these emotions that stop individuals/ teams performing.
3. If you were to choose 6 people from your company to work together on a special project, who, why and what type of energy would you want?

What Type of Learning Occurred For You?

- ☐ Awareness
- ☐ Skills
- ☐ Knowledge
- ☐ Insight
- ☐ Hindsight
- ☐ Foresight
- ☐ Technique
- ☐ Procedure
- ☐ Experience

Daily Record: A Sense of Yearning

1. Concepts/abstracts covered.

____

____

____

____

____

____

____

2. What do you want to use less and what is useful to you after the day's reading? Consider your behaviours, beliefs, thoughts, emotions, self-talk and values, for your own personal development as well as the development of staff and the company.

Personal Development

	Use less	Useful
Behaviours	____________	____________
Beliefs	____________	____________
Thoughts	____________	____________
Emotions	____________	____________
Self-talk	____________	____________
Values	____________	____________

Staff Development

	Use less	Useful
Behaviours	____________	____________
Beliefs	____________	____________
Thoughts	____________	____________
Emotions	____________	____________
Self-talk	____________	____________
Values	____________	____________

Company Development

	Use less	Useful
Behaviours	____________	____________
Beliefs	____________	____________
Thoughts	____________	____________
Emotions	____________	____________
Self-talk	____________	____________
Values	____________	____________

DAY 2: A SENSE OF PURPOSE
The notion of believing

People want direction. They don't want to be just busy all the time. They want to see themselves moving towards something. Because of our position in management, there are many ways to influence. We will be able to say to ourselves "How am I influencing, and how can I do it better?" The mere fact that we are the managers will mean that we have the power to influence.

Understanding the process of how we influence members in our team will be crucial for any team leader. People are influenced by patterns of attraction. Being attracted towards something actually sets a direction. What are people attracted to? If individuals are not sufficiently attracted to the team's objectives then they will move off and be distracted from the direction that has been set. As a manager, we have to guide individuals into those things which are useful and productive. So our job is to guide, educate and open up other possibilities.

We are all attracted to things. Often we are attracted to those things that are the same. We also know that many people are attracted to different situations or events. Something different, something exciting, or something new will hold their attention. However, our team members will not maintain this interest if they can't make sense out of what they are attending to. They like to be in charge of what goes on around them. They like to control the situation and own it.

We have to set up patterns of attraction so that employees possess or control the direction. The same occurs in relationships. We become attracted to someone and we can either control and possess the relationship, or change it to suit us, to alter it so that it fits with what we already know. Therefore, our job as managers is to create something different, to captivate and build an attraction so that we have a person's attention. From there we quickly scale this difference down, to something that team members are familiar with.

All companies have to grow or stand aside and allow others to take over. Most of us want to grow in the best possible way, and our sense of purpose keeps us on track. And we certainly are in command of what we believe in. However we can't have command unless there are people willing to be commanded. So our sense of purpose will be influenced by the relationships we create.

As we move into a relationship, we can begin to build for others their sense of purpose and their ability to believe in themselves. This is the greatest gift we can give to another, and will be at the heart of every project and every team. All of us want a connection, and we also want companionships.

We can relate to people in a variety of ways. We can shift between being serious and being playful. As team leaders we can be forceful and we can be more enticing. We can also re-connect individuals with their sense of purpose, if it seems that they have forgotten. We do this by building up another conflict inside them; a conflict with a direction that leads to resolution. For instance, "You can keep procrastinating all day long if you want to. This can be really annoying. But when you really get down to work, it's really nice to see you making decisions, and see how effective you are with our clients. Then I'm really impressed with what you can achieve."

We have to decide what we want. When we direct using our voice we are going to add more purpose. So we can build a sense of purpose which motivates the direction we have chosen. People have directions but they need a reason for doing the things that they do. As managers we can connect people to what matters to them. Remember that we have to make this reasonable. If we become unreasonable, we may become too angry with our staff, or if we get too seductive with them or too sweet with them, then they too may become unreasonable. When this occurs we can no longer influence with ease and elegance.

If we want to influence with elegance we must first begin with a belief that people can achieve. We want this belief to be fully operating, especially at the beginning of the week. Also at this time our managers can give individual attention to each co-ordinator. At the beginning of the week we are delivering instructions. We have a structure and the process about how to go about implementing this direction. We have a plan, but how do we deliver it? How much information do we want people to have?

We also have to consider how much we want to push and pull individuals into completing their tasks. How much influence do we want to have on this? The first Monday meeting is about delivering the direction for the coming week. We know that we are going to be marking out what needs to be completed and directing people into those areas that require attention.

Hopefully we can begin to leave team members with their own sense of purpose. Effective management usually means guiding people through what needs to be done once or twice. Then they should go and replicate the instructions and repeat them. They have then taken on our sense of direction. Being able to influence is an awesome ability if we want it. We can create the most amazing things, as long as we are clear on where or what it is that we want to do. There are so many beliefs that team members will have and so many things we have to deal with. So we have to choose what are the most useful beliefs that we wish to install. Sometimes we miss installing the beliefs that we believe are necessary for completing the project with ease. This is a natural oversight that probably often occurs within teams. This oversight also shows us that there is still more and more to learn.

The ultimate purpose in life is to discern what's constantly being added, what's changing and what's being refined. Life can be difficult at times, and we will have new challenges that we won't necessarily enjoy. They will test us to see what we are made of. Or we can go back to our routines, keeping things the same. That is certainly comfortable, but not necessarily fulfilling.

It is easy to have hindsight. Insight and foresight, however, are the real purpose of each experience and relationship, constructing those things we want, while avoiding those old patterns that detract from us and others. Actively being involved, giving and taking, and sharing are the things that build the magic. How we go about it is up to us. The options are plenty. We just need to allow our imagination to create something different, and then partake of it. Life is to be lived. There are people to meet, friends to be made, experiences to be enjoyed. We don't need a road map to do this. But we do need an attitude of abundance and plenty. Each of us has the same amount of time in a day, the same amount of energy and abilities, and the same amount of vulnerability. It's just what we choose to focus on.

The more we can involve people in the future of the company, the more they will see this future as their own. Gone are the days of subservience and control, for this only generates dependency. Employees need to know that management appreciates the worth of each individual within the team. They need to be reminded of their past successes, as well as what's ahead of them. As managers, we can also assist others in exploring what's possible in the future. Employees are often an under-rated investment. As an investment, it is up to us to be active in ensuring maximum returns.

Whatever we do, or wherever we find ourselves, there are so many things that we can extrapolate into other relationships in our lives. Details are important because they are the components that allow us to discern and figure out what we are experiencing. This builds choice and gives us the structure for our own sense of freedom. Being free within our own kingdom is the realm of what we make real and important to us. It is this process of abstraction that allows us to be unique, and ultimately the best we can be. This will be our sense of purpose that gives substance to our lives, and supports us through those daily obstacles, so that they are seen as hurdles, rather than insurmountable barriers.

Parameters of Purpose: Propelling Past and Compelling Future

Direction without purpose has little personal fulfilment. It is our purpose that makes things worthwhile. This is what inspires people to move, grow and reach their potential. People are motivated when they have a sense of purpose. We want them to be moving toward their future, producing in the present and building on their experience. To do this we have to make a propelling past and a compelling future. In other words, people are always moving away from something, and towards something else.

Propelling Past

Propelling is the process of keeping people going forward. One of the limitations of becoming an adult is about playing it safe. This can be because of family and social responsibilities. We tend to err on the side of caution rather than take too many risks. If we lose in business there is the possibility we may lose everything. So we have to be aware of people taking the safe option and just doing enough to get by. This is not useful when facing tomorrow.

All of us are different from what we were five years ago. There are many things in our past which we can laugh about. Whilst some feel guilt or shame about something that occurred, most people don't purposefully go out of their way to create these effects in life. Invariably, mistakes are made out of ignorance and not thinking through the consequences of our actions.

We have to constantly remind ourselves how individuals have developed when assessing their potential. Similarly, we have to remind others of their development; where they come from and where they are now. Putting past concerns behind us and extracting the learning from these events is not only useful, but also worthwhile in carrying on into the future. All of us have made mistakes and regret missed opportunities. We only have one life and we have to make the most of it. All of us have felt the awkwardness of understanding new skills. We have all had embarrassing moments, anxiety in taking risks, conflicts over choices, and our own personal stumbling blocks.

Playing it safe and doing more of the same only increases this anxiety. We have to teach people about cause and effect. That is, a past behaviour created an effect, and if this effect keeps occurring, it becomes a habit. So we effectively limit ourselves because of past fears. We become the effect, and find causes that justify our position. Perhaps some people are fortunate and are offered more opportunities. However, in most cases this isn't so. In the end, it is up to the individuals themselves. It is their decision if they choose to be continually affected by past events, and accept that this causes limitations in themselves, their family and their potential.

Doing things differently and seeking out new answers at least allows us to learn and break the habits that deceive us in the moment. Some have never considered the options that were available to them, or that they were a part of the larger picture. Their actions affect not only themselves but also others around them. As team managers our guidance will allow others to step out of the shackles of the past into a challenging future.

Compelling Future

We all have our dreams and hopes, not only for ourselves but also for our family and friends. What is the point in changing and going somewhere when it is uncertain, unpredictable and unknown? If we expect people to reach their potential then we have to assist them to see the benefits and become fully aware of the potency of a compelling future. If we build this future strongly enough it becomes the obvious passage to follow. Many companies use things such as incentives and rewards as a way of getting people to do more, but these eventually become redundant.

Although money motivates people some of the time, there are other things that they want. They need recognition for all the little things that they do and they require respect for who they are, what they face and what they are taking on. They need attention, support and encouragement. They need interest expressed in them, to remind them that they are reaching for something worthwhile. Very few people know what they want. That is why most of us set ourselves goals and outcomes. These become our focal point. They allow us to direct our energies. Usually it doesn't matter whether we actually achieve these targets, but the fact that there is a point to aim for, and a passage to explore.

As managers of a team we want people to arrive at a destination, and we also want to get there in a way that is productive not only to us, but to all team members. When we make the future absolutely compelling individuals want to move towards it. We do this by expanding the cause and effect model into effective causes. That is, we have to begin to describe the team's destination with enough details, so that it is alluring and seductive. We also have to highlight what individuals could miss out on, and therefore regret in the future, if they are not careful about how they go about things.

Ironically, the things that keep many people trapped, such as family and society, can also be the things that spur them on. The older we become the less we value money, because we have had time in the past to become more established. What replaces this value is the need for feeling worthwhile, meaning in our lives, esteem for the qualities we possess, so that we believe we contribute and are valued by those around us. When managing, we need to make a picture of the future to include all these things. Performing in one part of our life, at the expense of another, is a very short-term approach. For, if in the end, there is no one to share our achievements, we become lonely and question the value of what we have achieved. A compelling future balances all facets of our life. Assist others to know how far they have come, and how much further they need to go.

Case Study

A company I worked with was leading its market, had innovative services and was admired by others as a model of excellence. Yet it wasn't showing the returns it could. It had a clear direction, but was going about it in a way that was a reaction to its success. That is, they were just doing enough to remain in the lead, which was a guarantee for future failure. I was asked to work with their 12 junior managers.

Each of these managers was faced with the problem of getting those whom they managed to reach the company's targets and go beyond them. Senior management tried everything, from being supporting and encouraging, to being hard and demanding; all with very little effect.

My first question to the junior managers was "How did they decide upon a charity which they supported?" I told them that giving to others was useful, as long as they are prepared to pay the full price for doing this, and certainly not at someone else's expense. The company targets could be achieved with half a day's work, and senior management agreed that if the managers achieved their objectives, they could take the rest of the day off. After much discussion they decided that the charity was the service component of their job. This sounded reasonable, until we explored in the service of whom, and what for.

Encouraging and involving the junior managers in their own ideas of what service they were able to extend to others merely reiterated what senior management had been telling them all along. However, until this point, they had not believed sufficiently in other possibilities to actually implement them. They were caught in the dilemma of trying to reach their targets, rather than going beyond them. It was time for senior management to give up the charity of continually propping up these junior managers.

So, given the young managers had all the information they required, for the next three months they were on their own to work out and deliver strategies for achieving and going beyond their targets. Senior management were relieved at relinquishing their burden of constant support, and realised that this stepping back and allowing others to create their own compelling future would enable the junior managers to have faith and believe in their own ability, and an expectation that they could deliver the goods themselves.

That night the junior managers took the challenge and worked through what was required, for there is no day like tomorrow to begin. It was time for them to stand up and grow up. The very next day, not only did they hit their targets with ease, they were over 60 percent higher than the previous average for the year. These individuals believed in themselves, and now they had evidence to support this belief. The office changed the next day. There was a different energy. While the direction of the company was still the same, the junior managers now had a purpose; something to do, something to excel at. They believed in themselves. They also had a new charity – being accountable to each other and their teams, rather than themselves, and their previous excuses.

Transcript

Purpose is the reason for doing, achieving and giving meaning to our lives. It is interesting that work has become one of the major purposes in our life. In the distant past merely surviving was the key to our existence; surviving and continuing the race. We just looked after ourselves and our mates; making sure our family was warm around the fire, and at the end of the day enjoying the company of those around us. It was so simple then. Then again, so were we; uncomplicated, and unsophisticated. As time progressed, we found ourselves in a position of luxury where survival was no longer the prime concern. We now wanted something more than surviving.

We have an unquenchable thirst to explore, create and gain knowledge. We can question whether civilisation has really become civilised. Even pondering this question is a luxury in itself. It is easy to think back and moan about what our forefathers didn't do, or argue about what the new generation will expect. There is only one purpose that matters: yours. Your desires drive you to the destination which will become the legacy that others, such as your children and your children's children, will enjoy. Out of the chaos we create an order, a structure that allows us to live our lives for the better.

Australia is called the 'lucky country'. We are fortunate to have a stream of new people that arrive to take up the challenge of a new life and a new opportunity. With each new immigrant comes a passion and desire to achieve, not only for themselves, but for the next generation. This has all the hallmarks to guarantee success. These newcomers perceive the opportunities they have. They are prepared to work hard, and take risks. They have nothing to lose except the opportunity itself. They have, however, much to gain and they see all around them other individuals and other cultures that have established themselves. They see it and they want it. If we put our fears aside we can admire this, respect and welcome it, as it adds to all of us.

Most of us work for our children, and the legacy which we will leave them. We want to give them everything, however, if it's expected and accepted, they will inherit all our effort and we run the risk of making it too easy for them, so that the people we love the most lose their sense of purpose. There has to be greater goals other than ourselves and those immediate to us. This is why environmental concerns and issues of peace have become so important. And after these are nourished and fulfilled, what will be the next purpose for getting out of bed in the morning?

The same is true with our companies. Each year people risk their dreams and believe enough in themselves to work at creating something. The majority will fail but that won't stop them, because there is a wealth of opportunities and experiences to be gained. Often companies become too big and complacent and lose their purpose. Too many people get to the point in life where they feel they have missed out; what is the purpose, there's got to be something else? Well, there is! It's the next project, because projects have the wonderful ability of taking us into the future, where challenges abound and opportunities await.

Exercise of Day 2: A Sense of Purpose

Extraordinary

Usefulness

1. Making new things exciting.
2. Placing challenges others can reach.
3. Requiring and demanding more.

Concepts to Be Remembered

- Actions speak louder than words.
- We can't live off the past forever.
- People need a destination and a way of getting there.
- Purpose is powerful.
- Surprise and delight yourself as well as others.

Steps

1. Every person has a story that is extraordinary. Think of your team members. What is extraordinary about them? What do they excel at?
2. What would be an extraordinary experience to have within your team?
3. Set up the experience. Demand or challenge team members to work towards this.
4. How will you be extraordinary and not just another manager?

What Type of Learning Occurred For You?

☐ Awareness	☐ Skills	☐ Knowledge
☐ Insight	☐ Hindsight	☐ Foresight
☐ Technique	☐ Procedure	☐ Experience

Daily Record: A Sense of Purpose

1. Concepts/abstracts covered.

____

____

____

____

____

____

2. What do you want to use less and what is useful to you after the day's reading? Consider your behaviours, beliefs, thoughts, emotions, self-talk and values, for your own personal development as well as the development of staff and the company.

Personal Development

	Use less	**Useful**
Behaviours	________	________
Beliefs	________	________
Thoughts	________	________
Emotions	________	________
Self-talk	________	________
Values	________	________

Staff Development

	Use less	Useful
Behaviours	____________	____________
Beliefs	____________	____________
Thoughts	____________	____________
Emotions	____________	____________
Self-talk	____________	____________
Values	____________	____________

Company Development

	Use less	Useful
Behaviours	____________	____________
Beliefs	____________	____________
Thoughts	____________	____________
Emotions	____________	____________
Self-talk	____________	____________
Values	____________	____________

DAY 3: A SENSE OF READINESS
The notion of being prepared

As with many things in life, being ready allows us to excel at what we do best. As managers, time spent in preparation is time well spent, for it allows the team to do the task at hand. If we know our outcome or the messages that we are continually projecting to others, we can also predict some of those things that might happen. This allows us to be prepared for some of these eventualities. Ultimately we need to resource the team, and ensure that the team's resources are available to all team members.

With the building of a sense of yearning and purpose we can now get down to the logistics of what's required, such as who's involved, what part each individual plays, how these people connect with each other, what time frames are applicable, what equipment and funds are required, and which supplies are available. Giving adequate time to ensure and plan that these things are dealt with and organised enables others to be concerned with their part in the whole project. It also makes the success of the project more plausible, so that it becomes a reality, rather than just an idea.

No matter what we do, we will leave an impression; an impression that lasts. Hopefully the impression which we leave will be one that adds to the another person. When we are in a state of readiness, we have prepared, as best we can, for every contingency. We are then more astute at seeing an opportunity when it comes our way as well as dealing with the unexpected. The journey of our project becomes more manageable and predictable. Remember, time and time again, it's the little things that count. And as they add up, for they surely will, it is these little pieces that build the structure of tomorrow. Elegance occurs everywhere. In each and every one of us, there is a part to play. Often, however, we only appreciate the significance of a person's contribution when they are no longer there.

In preparing for any endeavour, sometimes we can take ourselves too seriously. Stop and say to yourself, "How useful is this to me?" And more importantly, "How does this add to those people around me?" And then just smile. When we have done this, we have begun the process of becoming our best! This is probably the most prepared we can be. It is just so easy. We can set ourselves free from our own constraints. Build a set of expectations, rather than merely pleasing others and their expectations. When we please ourselves we find we are actually pleasing others who are important to us. Just enjoy a moment in time, for that is all we have in this life. To be fully prepared, begin with a belief that utilises all the resources which we have available to us:

"I think I can!

I know I can!

Of course I can!"

Yes, of course we can because we have a purpose and a will that is as strong as steel, and uniquely ours. It belongs to us and no one else. This sense of purpose will keep us on target, and will allow us to enjoy preparing for the project, to ensure that all details are considered. Nothing is overlooked. That's why relationships are important for they allow us to share these experiences, to work together, gain opinions from others on the best course of action, and anticipate and overcome difficulties thoroughly and expediently.

In everything we do, in every situation we find ourselves in, we make a connection. We draw from our experiences and our relationships, those things that matter. For most of the time it is the little things, those daily distractions, that may appear trivial or insignificant when seen in isolation. But when each and every one of these are drawn together, they determine the significance of our project. They can actually add substance and sustenance that enrich our life. Being prepared is attending to the little things. By doing this, the big issues generally take care of themselves.

There will be things which we may not have prepared for. We are not going to get it right every time, every day. Some days we just get too involved in ourselves, so we relate to others through a filter of our own issues and overlook the obvious things that require attention. We need to put our issues to one side. When we do this we can focus on the task directly ahead of us. This is an ability which all competent and professional teams must master.

One way we can assist others to remain focused when preparing for a project is to offer them choice. This gives team members options and builds a personal sense of freedom in determining how best to prepare for what is ahead. If we have choice, we believe we have a say in our lives. We can begin to take more responsibility because if we own the work we do, it's ours. Then we become accountable for the consequences.

Most times, however, it is an illusion of choice, since directives mostly come down from above. Management has set the direction. We, in turn, can develop our sense of readiness when we have choices in how these directives will be implemented. There is always choice in how we deliver the goods. It's about how people are going to leave their individual stamp and how they are going to do their job. Some individuals thrive on challenge, others like things to be more predictable. Some like it tough, some like it easy. But we all like to do it in our own style.

Selection of the individuals who will participate in the project is important, however, choosing those people who continually shine in their performance is not crucial. A team of stars can be difficult to manage. Many teams have won premierships without stars. Most people actually produce more when giving for others, because others believe in them. They are steady and solid in their work, which in itself creates its own brilliance. Selecting individuals to become team players requires a sorting process which will identify the right blend of resources, skills and personal traits which will allow all members to work together, and the specific criteria needed for the team leader.

Parameters of Readiness: Organisation and Astuteness

Being ready is a state of being that builds its own momentum. This is crucial so that the project not only gets off to a good start, but is also thought through to determine what is needed, right through to its completion. As managers, we need to create the parameters of readiness, so that team members have the ability to be flexible and fluid in the team's progress. These parameters include organisation and astuteness.

Organisation

Organisation requires making a judgement. Ascertaining what will be useful allows the team to identify what they will gain and what will be the cost of engaging in the current behaviour. We may save time by being involved but we can also reduce the learning that might be useful for the next project. It is more powerful to assist people in becoming more actively involved. They will only do this if they can see the opportunities, and believe they have the ability and permission to implement an action which they consider useful to the project's successful conclusion. In this regard, managers are service providers to the rest of the team, ensuring that team members have enough direction to allow them to make decisions for themselves.

In other words, team leaders need to keep individuals ready by focusing them on their tasks or the job at hand. Managing is about anticipating the myriad of things that require attention and not taking the limelight of the project. This enables the team leader to show support by involving and assisting others. Major problems and challenges can be open for discussion or suggestions, and invariably will require the team leader to make the decision. Making decisions are easy if we have considered at least three options, and appreciate why we have chosen one option over another possibility. As long as we base our decision on the purpose and fundamental beliefs of the team, we will go forward with the support of the majority.

Smooth operation and organisation will require that decisions be made over a variety of areas. These areas require that the team leader oversee the decisions made and involve the necessary skills to maximise success. The areas of service that need to be considered and followed through are:

1. Supplies – What to order, how much and when.
2. Administration and paper work and being accountable, which also assists planning of the next project.
3. Sourcing for outside assistance and information to make the task easier.
4. Storage and accessibility, to ensure the flow and continuation of the project.

5. Liaison to see senior managers and other interested parties.
6. Planning and preparing marketing and advertising, to promote the product either internally or externally.
7. Arranging of transport, such as removal and storage to the end user.
8 Co-ordination between the project and the company, so that the project blends in with harmony, and doesn't disrupt other company functions and projects.
9. Intervention and interjection to solve disputes, clarify issues and actively assist others to find solutions.
10. Safety and health issues. Consult with relative departments, such as fire, civil defence, and workcare. This promotes care, reduces concerns and shows consideration.

When we consider all the logistics that need to be implemented, we increase the team's ability to be ready for the unexpected. We may not have identified every contingency, but most have been anticipated.

Astuteness

While being ready assists us to plan for most contingencies, being astute allows us to see opportunities as they arise, and create future possibilities which will enable the team to reach its full potential. The ability to pursue and grow in the following areas ensures, not only the project's successful conclusion, but that the team and manager will also personally grow and develop. We need to master our internal self, to be able to put ourselves aside if necessary, connect with other team members, and utilise the qualities to the fullest when required. To become more astute we need to consider:

Being Sensible

Being sensible is to have the ability to perceive things and use our senses to remain alert for those things which we want to track. Perceptions are altered by our beliefs. What we gather information on will determine what we remain open to. When we decide something is important, this is most likely to be the area where we will gather the most information. Therefore, how we sort information will determine what we search for. And what we search for invariably we will find. However, when we gather more information, from a variety of sources, we have the ability to develop a multitude of perspectives to give us greater insight.

Being Believable

What we believe sets the parameters of what we think is possible. Once having established the overriding beliefs of a project, we need to adhere to these beliefs to ensure our credibility. As managers, through preparedness, we take what is considered possible and turn this into something which is plausible. We do this by giving what we think is possible a detailed structure and a way of achieving it. Both the costs and gains of the project need to be researched and resourced, and even if the project has a ten percent success rate, at least that ten percent is solid to work from.

Being Stable

Being stable relates to building powerful and strong emotions that add to the richness of our experiences. We can allow other people to accommodate to what is happening around them, since too much change too quickly builds uneasy feelings that things are becoming unpredictable. As managers, remember enthusiasm can come in many forms, however, it needs to be consistent throughout the project. At other times, determination and persistence can be injected to ensure that enthusiasm for the team's goals does not waver.

Being Accountable

Our thinking has to be taken into account when we plan for something. The project's aim has to be thought through and presented in a manner which others can understand. As managers, we have to be astute and think in different ways to acknowledge what is important to each team member, and so translate our objectives in a way that has meaning for each member. We also need to make provision for the unexpected by generating contingency plans.

Being Adaptable

Being adaptable is the ability to move in and out of the group, to display a variety of behaviours that signal to the rest of the team how they are performing. A variety of styles is needed if we are to successfully connect with each member: sometimes relaxed, sometimes pushy, but always maintaining the momentum and focus.

Case Study

The challenge was to participate in the 50th anniversary of the Sydney to Hobart yacht race. From initial discussions to arriving at a decision, it took two months. It began with a good friend of mine wanting to take part in the race. Initially his aim was to get a place on someone's boat. The possibility was raised of entering our own boat. As the discussions continued our plans would change by the hour, from the size and shape of the boat to who would be involved and how we would find it.

We located a boat in Hong Kong, a 51-foot cruiser that would require substantial work to get it ready by December. Other people were free with their criticisms and concerns, and these had an effect. It wasn't until we decided what our overriding beliefs were, and stuck to these, that we made any headway.

The most important belief we had was that we wanted to participate; winning wasn't important. Secondly, we wanted to do our best. Thirdly, we would get a crew together; people with a passion for sailing and create an experience that everyone would remember. We found an old boat in Sydney and began the process of working out what was required in the way of equipment, people and sponsorship.

The only real resource we had was a yearning to complete the race. We sourced and searched the world, looking for a crew, to gather together the people able to complete the race. We required specific skills, but more importantly an attitude, which was a love for the sea and the ability to share this with others. We also had the boat pulled out of the water and surveyed to evaluate its worthiness for such a voyage.

We even consulted a Chinese numerologist to check out whether the energy of the boat was right. Advice was given not to purchase anything that was moving, such as a car or boat. It was all right to do the race, however, we now had to look at other options, find a sponsor or go for joint ownership by the crew. This opened up another set of possibilities which had to be explored. No matter what, the answers are there if you search diligently. To date, we are preparing for the next stage of the planning, regardless of the surveyor's report or finance. We are preparing what equipment is required, the work that needs to be done, and the people to bring together for five days of racing.

The experience of the race itself, the involvement in a team, and the success of being across that finishing line are all part of creating a memory and facing the personal challenge with other people. To gather a group of strangers together for a competition requires some consideration. As a team, Mother Nature will challenge us. Together the idea is a little closer.

Transcript

Every day we are faced with demands and expectations. How ready are we for them? How open we are to doing something different? In just one moment our life can change. We can meet somebody or do something that challenges our reality. This will require that we cope in a new way.

The nice thing about projects and why they are so powerful is that they allow us to direct our attention and develop our abilities, to meet and overcome a challenge. This give us purpose. While each day requires that we do many things which are the same, there are many things we can extract from our experiences. Being part of life is about being ready. This does not mean we spend all our time preparing for what might happen. It's more about embracing an opportunity, giving ourselves choices and believing in those resources which could be possible.

One of the reasons why our potential is often hidden is that people don't challenge themselves. How do we know what we can do, until we begin to do it? Life is a series of projects, or perhaps just one big project with many parts to it. A ship without any heading is at sea. Without purpose of moving from one point to another, she is just cruising. Without proper maintenance and provisions she is at the mercy of whatever Mother Nature can throw at her. As we face our future these principles apply for each of us. Business can't predict fully the economic weather. We can only forecast and be right some of the time. Those businesses which are ready for possibilities can respond and react with a freedom that can allow them to race off with the prize.

The most successful airline in Asia has a pool of staff, from management all the way down, who are in training for two months. All staff will be rotated through this training. This pool of staff becomes a resource at the ready, so that the company can move with a quick response to an opportunity. The same occurs with specialist units in the armed forces and civil defence, so that emergencies can be counteracted as quickly as possible.

A small company has asked me how to have a similar pool of staff because they liked the concept. We decided to select two staff per one hundred employees, and train them in the generalist skills of managing a project or a team. This group would be rotated throughout the company, so there will always be people ready to adapt and be accountable for opportunity.

Initially this was seen as not productive. However, this process will free up individuals to plan future projects. In addition, it has the added benefits of actively showing the staff that the future is worth planning for, and that developmental programmes are a worthwhile pursuit.

Being prepared starts from within, for what you do today in business will not be required tomorrow. Not everyone can become leaders but we can all become involved.

Exercise of Day 3: A Sense of Readiness

Of course you can

Usefulness

1. Becoming capable in doing new things.
2. Sourcing new abilities.
3. Stretching and challenging ourselves.

Concepts to Be Remembered

- Of course you can!
- Excuses are either can't, won't, couldn't, wouldn't.
- Being stable may undermine your flexibility.
- Adapting is the key to success.

Steps

1. Set a problem at work that seems insurmountable.
2. Create a strategy to deal with this difficulty. What new things do you have to learn or do?
3. Work out the component parts and the process to learn these new processes or skills.
4. How do you refine this process? What shortcuts will be useful? How can you make the refinements more natural?

What Type of Learning Occurred For You?

☐ Awareness	☐ Skills	☐ Knowledge
☐ Insight	☐ Hindsight	☐ Foresight
☐ Technique	☐ Procedure	☐ Experience

Daily Record: A Sense of Readiness

1. Concepts/abstracts covered.

____

____

____

____

____

____

2. What do you want to use less and what is useful to you after the day's reading? Consider your behaviours, beliefs, thoughts, emotions, self-talk and values, for your own personal development as well as the development of staff and the company.

Personal Development

	Use less	**Useful**
Behaviours	__________	__________
Beliefs	__________	__________
Thoughts	__________	__________
Emotions	__________	__________
Self-talk	__________	__________
Values	__________	__________

Staff Development

	Use less	**Useful**
Behaviours	__________	__________
Beliefs	__________	__________
Thoughts	__________	__________
Emotions	__________	__________
Self-talk	__________	__________
Values	__________	__________

Company Development

	Use less	Useful
Behaviours	____________	____________
Beliefs	____________	____________
Thoughts	____________	____________
Emotions	____________	____________
Self-talk	____________	____________
Values	____________	____________

DAY 4: A SENSE OF INVOLVEMENT
The notion of belonging

People want to have a say in what they are doing, which is different from being in charge of what they are doing. Most of us realise that somebody has to make the decisions and be responsible for the overall project. This, in itself, is quite reassuring. In other words, people will follow what they believe are good, sound decisions. They are prepared to go along with someone, and be part of a team or project when they believe in what they are doing. Therefore, involving someone is a way of acknowledging their importance and showing them that their contribution is worthwhile. Being part of something is powerful because it allows us to connect with others, challenge our own beliefs and test our skills and abilities.

The old adage of "a little goes a long way" is important, not only for those doing the work required, but also for keeping everyone involved. Asking people's opinions and suggestions is crucial in maintaining this flow. The skills of a manager come to the fore when sorting through these suggestions and opinions. Collecting these points of view not only gives us a great deal of information about understanding each member of the team, but also provides ample opportunities to facilitate learning and highlight useful experiences for all involved. Therefore, suggestions and opinions shouldn't be dismissed, but rather acknowledged and evaluated according to their merit in assisting the team towards a speedy and efficient completion of the project.

All team members will have opinions. These judgements will be based on a criteria which assists individuals in sorting through information. By having this criteria, we can begin to understand and relate with others, according to the judgements we have made. However, in too many cases, we tend to make a personal stand over issues that may not be directly relevant, since many of these opinions are based on digital sorting processes:

Digital Processes	**Source**
Good/Bad	Parents
Right/Wrong	School
In/Out	Peers
Yes/No	Authority figures
Innocent/Guilty	Judicial system
Success/Failure	Business
Appropriate/Inappropriate	Society
On/Off	Technology
Black/White	Religion
True/False	Education
Trusting/Distrusting	Relationships

These digital (that is, either/or) judgements can destroy relationships and individual potential very rapidly. We are more than one or the other. We are capable of having a combination of these qualities and also capable of being inconsistent. Difficulties usually arise when we become too certain, and in most cases, too final. Most people who are unpredictable and multifaceted in their responses cannot, and will not, allow themselves to be judged in this way.

By contrast, sorting information using an analogical process allows us to make small, incremental shifts in our opinions, rather than the "on/off" approach of digital processing. Analogue processing is a more useful way when leading a team, since we can extract the value or usefulness from every idea presented, rather than totally dismissing opinions presented to us. Individuals are not categorised by "black or white" descriptions, but are seen more realistically as having a variety of responses and personal qualities. Some of these responses and qualities may need to be used less, since they interfere with the team's progression, while others will need to be used more fully, since these responses support the team's development and success. As team leaders, we want to remember that all individuals have worth and potential. Therefore, we want to be constantly sorting for the usefulness in any opinion we have or approach that we take:

What's useful here?

What do I need to use less? ← → **What do I need to use more fully?**

↓

How can I extract the usefulness of this?

In the world of business, we need a better system that frees our thinking and behaviour, so we can go for more challenges. Many business successes are built by people doing things that went against the majority's opinion. For example, these individuals ignored the warnings of "It's impossible," "It can't be done," "It's not the right way," or "They said that shouldn't happen." Instead, these leaders determined what was useful for their customers, and determined the usefulness of their product or service, so it can then be used more fully. This incorporates all three components of:

Change	**Growth**	**Development**
(Useful)	*(Usefulness)*	*(Use fully)*

With these processes we can not only be successful in planning business, but also have the approach to maintain this success. Each process requires separate skills and strategies. Implementing these strategies becomes easier when we constantly ask ourselves "How is what we are doing useful, what do we need to use more fully, and what do we want to use less of?" When we ask these questions we open up possibilities in our business world, and go beyond the limits we have placed upon ourselves and those around us.

No matter what we are doing we will have experiences. From these experiences we need to determine what we keep and enjoy, and what we leave behind us. Or else we take everything on board and have to cope with the lot and deal with all our baggage! If we are not careful, we build for ourselves future worries, concerns and doubts. We generalise these anxieties to describe our entire future, so we have only bleakness to look forward to! When personalising our experiences too much, we have to relate to them again and again.

Parameters of Involvement: Active and Passive

Business people need to take risks, set challenges and drive forward into new ventures. When we sort for what is useful, and take the learning from the experiences we have, we become more active in the way we relate with ourselves and others, rather than just passively responding to the world around us. Knowing when to be actively involved and when to take more of a back seat is crucial in the development of the project and the function of the team. There will be times, however, when we want to be passive, and not automatically step in to resolve and rescue individuals from their problems and difficulties.

Active

To be resourceful we need to actively identify what resources we have available to us. It may seem like a strange question – but what are resources? Some are natural, some are learned and some are still possible. They include skills, knowledge, qualities, experiences, learning, beliefs and emotions, cultural values, and finally, techniques.

In making an inventory of our own personal resources, we have the opportunity to gain more from our own personal wealth. We can start the process of becoming more resourceful by asking ourselves 3 questions:

1. How can I adapt this resource to do something else?
2. How can I become more adept at this?
3. What else can I adopt that will make this more resourceful?

In preparing the team to deliver their best we need to be aware of the vastness of resources that people have to offer, and how to utilise these.

Natural	Learned	Possible
Qualities	Skills	Experiences
Traits	Knowledge	Thoughts
Likes	Techniques	Dreams
Disposition	Beliefs	Desires
Emotions	Experiences	Emotions
	Habits	

It may take some time to catalogue all available resources, but it becomes a useful personal profile, rather than a test. If we are to direct and develop people we need a good database to work from. By knowing which resources people have, we can activate the parts that are relevant and build the connections that coordinate a team's effort. In addition, this inventory will also build an individual's self-worth. We have more than we imagine, yet often we fail to acknowledge what we have.

This potential is about hidden talent. Nothing is insignificant unless we deem it to be. When we use our resources effectively we can set a series of challenges to a group of people. When they combine their hidden talents with the task that needs to be done, they can go far beyond their expectations. The pre-project briefing should include this information. When planning to utilise our resources we need to ask the following questions:

1. What resources will be needed?
2. Who will deliver them, and what expectations will be given to these people?
3. When they will be involved?
4. Where are their talents and energy best needed?

As managers we need to work out how to involve all people, in a variety of different ways, other than just their speciality. When we do this, we are resourcing the resources!

Passive

Often when we think of passive behaviour we conjure up a negative image, mainly because managers have tried for years to actively encourage people to take a more participatory role. Ironically, in doing so they have actually created passivity because people learn to wait to be motivated. So if we solve all their problems at work, the team comes to rely on the leader to deal with any issue that arises. At times we need to stand back and allow people the opportunity to take charge of their project.

When expectations are clear and planning has been thorough, so that each person knows what is required of them, the role of the manager becomes one of servicing and assistance. Each time we find ourselves drawn into moment management we need to give ourselves more options. Ask the questions, "By doing this, what do I reinforce?", "What do team members learn?", "What else could I be doing?", "By not intervening, what is the worse thing that could happen?" and finally, "By not intervening, how will their outcome be different to mine?". If expediency is important, then become involved because this tells us that our planning was insufficient. Learn from this for the next time.

The quickest way of getting others involved is to show them or model the experience or task which is required. Particularly during the initial stages of the project, team leaders will need to work closely with people, so they know exactly how and what to do. We need to deliver clear directives and statements about what we consider useful, and provide explanations when we impose our presence on others without question. In many instances, it will require pointing out what others may have missed. Reduce ignorance by making people more aware.

Interest, curiosity and intrigue are the doorways to awareness. When we ask questions and display these qualities to others it not only makes them feel involved, but also gives them the means to become more involved themselves. Identify simple cause and effect processes. That is, for everything that happens there is a cause, and that most effects are responsible for causing something, somewhere. Teaching people not to be just reactive requires that they be aware that individual causes can affect the whole team.

Therefore, as managers, anticipate and plan who will directly or inadvertently affect another member of the team. All team members form links in a chain. The strength of the chain is determined by the weakest link. Strengthen these weak links by providing individuals with respect and recognition for their qualities and skills, and support and reassurance for their learning and uncertainties.

The more people claim ownership of the project, the more they will play a part in its delivery. As managers, we can stand back and become more passive, so that all members of the team can connect with each other. It's important that we make clear each primary role; that we can assist and guide rather than dominate and control. The more they are involved, the more they gain from the project.

Case Study

Irene, a 32-year-old supervisor of operations, was excellent in doing her job, to the extent that she was hard to replace. The company was thinking of expanding and promoting Irene in the organisation, but felt that if they removed her from operations, her department would suffer. Irene definitely ran a tight ship. She knew all facets of operations and could complete any task with competence and ease. The problem was that no one else could do her job, so there was no one who could succeed her. In other words, she made herself indispensable. The company could employ an outsider, but this too would effect operations. So she was bypassed again for the promotion, with her only crime being she did her job really well.

Everybody liked and depended on Irene. She took personal pride and integrity in ensuring the job was completed thoroughly. Often this would mean staying back after the others had left the office to personally finish the job. In other words, she completed what the other employees had left unfinished. Under closer examination, cause and effect patterns were identified. Experienced staff members were not working to their potential. These individuals knew how to do enough, and were happy just to get by.

Irene had been excellent in teaching junior staff how they too could do enough. The first thing I proposed to Irene was the notion of self-management. She had concerns and still wanted to check if the job was adequately finished. She also feared that people would take advantage of the situation if she did not continue to monitor and check up on the completed tasks. She knew that the senior staff were not striving to do more, and this only fuelled her fears. While total self-management is the way of the future, it does, however, require a dramatic change in thinking and ways of managing.

So Irene and I came back from this extreme change, and came up with the concept of full service, where each member of operations was trained in the activities and functions of other members of the department. This would make other team players more involved and give them more responsibility. Initially people were not enthusiastic about this, because Irene was their excuse of "This was just a job, where you did your bit and got paid." After about six months it became evident who were the charity cases within her division of operations. Her decision was now to cull or change the charities. Two of the staff took up the challenge and are now being groomed to replace Irene.

Planning to be passive and allowing others to pick up the load freed Irene to do the things she really enjoyed. Rather than actually doing the work she formulated a plan for meeting the others half way. Supervision was given on handling enquiries and answering questions which might arise. Those who wanted to learn had to show their interest and motivation. The more they did this, the more encouragement they received. It's not enough doing your job, it's ensuring that your skills and experience are passed on, so you can move onto the next step.

Transcript

The ingredients that make people feel like they belong are trust, loyalty, interest and respect. The biggest factor that stops these things being fulfilled are individual beliefs and fears. Too many managers are into control and power. They demonstrate this through their position of territory and are not prepared to hand over some of the responsibility and tasks that are necessary for personal development. Not relinquishing territory stunts a person's growth, because they appear busy and always in charge. Most individuals will only hand over when change demands it, which usually comes from above or from outside the company.

In reality, people don't want the project dumped on them, particularly with very little preparation and resources available. So it is the wise manager who will create more time. Make the most of the people you have to work with. You have to be able to manage people, not control them. If the philosophy of the company is to expand and grow, then people need to be involved in the early stages so that they can own these changes. You can live by fears, control and checking up on others, and mistakes will possibly be reduced. But that is where you remain, a checker, a worrier and a doubter.

Certainly people make mistakes. However, we know that this is one of the best ways to learn. More importantly, people deserve faith in their work. How else can they reach their potential? In addition, effective managers free themselves from the daily operations of the company. This allows them time to dream and explore future directions for the organisation. So there is a balance between preparing yourself and preparing the team. Be ready for any eventuality.

If management is too tight, people don't need to be involved. They don't need to think, they just need to do. So many managers say that they haven't got enough time in the day, and that they wish workers would show more initiative and common sense. My question to them is always: "What is it about your style that creates compliance, rather than involvement?" Managers who manage territories are really doing it for themselves and saving face, and are not interested in the workers and their potential. They are more interested in fulfilling their own needs. Ultimately, managers only need to be around to open up new business, receive directives from above, service their team, and become a consultant in the whole process.

Being active and managing in a way that enhances the team will actually enhance the manager. Businesses are made either by those who create the initiatives, those who are freed to develop the work, and those who service thoroughly. How you actively work towards these processes also makes the job more exciting and interesting. Rather than work from a checklist of what must be done, you are focusing on making sound judgements, which not only develops your workers, but yourself as well. You are adding to tomorrow's management. With self-management not too far away, those managers who manage themselves and their personal style are the ones that will fly.

Exercise of Day 4: A Sense of Involvement

Taking action

Usefulness

1. Taking charge and forging a path.
2. Learning from feedback.
3. Promoting ownership of the project.

Concepts to Be Remembered

- Fortune favours the brave.
- Risks make success. Ownership is having a say in something.
- Adopt a new strategy.
- Adapt and learn from feedback.
- Become adept by refining what you have learned.

Steps

1. Consider an aspect of your competitor's product or service that is superior when compared with your company.
2. Become active:

   What could you adopt into your company?

   How could you adapt this service to suit your customers?

   What needs to be refined, so that it becomes more natural?
3. How will customers and staff be indirectly affected by these changes?

What Type of Learning Occurred For You?

☐ Awareness	☐ Skills	☐ Knowledge
☐ Insight	☐ Hindsight	☐ Foresight
☐ Technique	☐ Procedure	☐ Experience

Daily Record: A Sense of Involvement

1. Concepts/abstracts covered.

____

____

____

____

____

____

2. What do you want to use less and what is useful to you after the day's reading? Consider your behaviours, beliefs, thoughts, emotions, self-talk and values, for your own personal development as well as the development of staff and the company.

Personal Development

	Use less	**Useful**
Behaviours	__________	__________
Beliefs	__________	__________
Thoughts	__________	__________
Emotions	__________	__________
Self-talk	__________	__________
Values	__________	__________

Staff Development

	Use less	**Useful**
Behaviours	________	________
Beliefs	________	________
Thoughts	________	________
Emotions	________	________
Self-talk	________	________
Values	________	________

Company Development

	Use less	**Useful**
Behaviours	________	________
Beliefs	________	________
Thoughts	________	________
Emotions	________	________
Self-talk	________	________
Values	________	________

DAY 5: A SENSE OF RESOLVE
The notion of durability

At some stage of the project it is going to get tough. It is going to require more from our team than they can deliver in the moment. When this occurs individual resolve and durability will be tested. It will be different for each member, as each person reacts and responds to the pressures placed upon them. This is the true guideline for testing whether a project will be challenged or stretched.

As managers we need to keep track of the amount of tension and stress that these challenges bring. The symptoms of when our resolve is being tested will include uncertainty, irritation, avoidance, boredom and fatigue. When this occurs individuals have to 'dig deep' and find that bit extra. All the preparation of being ready, and understanding people's resources, allows the manager to connect team members with their personal qualities and other facets of themselves which will assist them when the going becomes tough.

The easy option for people when obstacles seem insurmountable is to capitulate and be overcome by the experience. This is brought on by individuals doubting their own ability, or not having faith in what's possible for themselves and the team. As a manager we need to orientate each of these experiences to something different and more useful. We do this through our language. We can shift any pattern through the beginning, by identifying and showing how well people have done up until now, or move team members to the ending by talking about what it will be like when the project is completed or finished. By shifting to different parts of the experience we can ease the tension of the moment. We have the ability to distract people from themselves, if they are too serious about what is currently happening in the team.

As managers, we need to do this quickly, quietly and effectively. Together we can face anything and overcome any difficulty if we trust our judgements. Rather than rushing, solving and doing for others, we can use our language elegantly and effectively to direct them to their own resources, beliefs and personal strengths.

Language

As managers we can use our language to direct staff through an experience. This requires that we become precise in our communication, to move people forward, towards completion and celebration. Similarly, we can track employees by their use of language, since this will indicate where they are in the experience.

Words that we can use to assist an individual through an experience will include:

Beginning	**Middle**	**Ending**
Start	Progressive	Found
Begin	Continuing	Over
New	On-going	Finished
First	During	Complete
Initial	Moving	Resolution
Fresh	Striving	Outcome
Early	Reaching	Conclusion
Foremost	Finding	Finally
Innovative	Seeking	Arrived
Add 5 more:	**Add 5 more:**	**Add 5 more:**

Behaviours

Trust requires that we have faith. This is a belief in something, without specific evidence to support this belief. When we have faith and trust in our workers we go beyond limiting beliefs, and people endure and overcome amazing obstacles. What we want is useful behaviour, not emotions or beliefs which get in the way. Therefore, we have to show trust and display this to others in our actions and words. When individuals believe they are trusted and that someone has faith in them, the old expression of "people going to hell and back" is demonstrated in the team. We do not want to let down those who believe in us.

Behaviours are a part of every experience. These actions will be different at the beginning, middle and end of an experience. Once again, some behaviours will limit the individual progressing through the experience, so that they remain stuck, while other behaviours will enhance the experience.

Beginning	**Middle**	**End**
Limit – *Unnatural*	**Limit** – *Unco-ordinated*	**Limit** – *Incomplete*
Awkward/Jerky	Easily distracted	Incomplete actions
Tentative	Not followed through	Not smooth
Larger movements	Short cuts	Cumbersome
Unco-ordinated	Too much/Too little	Out of place
Too fast/Too slow	Repetitive/Redundant	Taper off
Enhance – *Natural*	**Enhance** – *Co-ordinated*	**Enhance** – *Elegance*
Comfortable with self	Just do it	Gracefulness
Steadiness	Accommodate	Style
Good posture	Refine, less gross	Well-rounded
Work form centre out	Finer movements	End is clear and precise
Going out to meet others	Explore variations	Purpose and result
Too much or too little	Economical movements	Measured
In right direction	Move to complex tasks	Natural

Beginning	Middle	End
Behaviours of trust	**Behaviours of trust**	**Behaviours of trust**
Building credibility – the testing phase	Little things matter	Involvement, closer fun
Solid	Partaking, sharing	Working together
Open and expanding	Going out and exploring	Intimate, consistent
Extending	Embracing other ideas	Reliability, dependable
Warmth	Do different things	Not intrusive, relaxed
Smile	Ask questions and listen	At ease with others' space
Friendliness	Share/give alternatives	Can challenge another
Easy	Embrace learning	Joint rhythm, in sync
No jerkiness	Ask when we want something	Differences are respected
Not too fast/too slow	Less gross – smaller movements (*adaptable*)	What we do is admired
		People ask us questions
		Bring up problems
		Laughter, acknowledges

Knowing where we ended with trust at the last meeting with another, assists us in picking up where we left off, rather than going back to the beginning. For most people, if we break trust we have to go right back to the beginning. Trust will be different for each person we meet, and there are many different forms of trust to explore. Each person has their own structure of demonstrating trust, fuelled by their beliefs and values.

Parameters of Resolve: Minimise and Maximise

We can adopt the simple paradigm that all we need to do is maximise some behaviours, and minimise others. The least we can do is our best. If that is not enough, then we need to adopt something else. People have the resources to overcome anything, because somewhere, someone has thought of the challenge that we face. However, we may not be going about it the right way and be tempted to give in too soon.

Minimise

Firstly we need to identify the symptoms of the behaviour which we want to reduce, and we must start with ourselves. We need to minimise the effects we are creating, and become aware of our doubts, concerns and fears. Anxiety is contagious. It either comes from us or we can pick it up from others. We need to minimise these behaviours by reassuring ourselves and others.

We need to question our own decisions in a useful way that adds to ourselves, rather than deleting our own pool of resources. When we question or are faced with a decision, we can begin to ask questions that can give us some of the answers. Some of these questions are "Where else would this be useful?", "Who else can assist?" and "How else can we do this?". In times of doubt, we can revert back to our fundamental beliefs and purpose for doing the work we do. We can also remind ourselves where we are going, how far off track we may have wandered, and how much further we need to go. Being open will assist us in this process: "What if we did this?" Do this personally, before sharing it with the team, so when answers are required we can provide them. If we keep searching we will find the answers.

Minimise long periods of work where people are focused on one specific job. If people are irritated or stuck don't keep them doing the same tasks. Direct them to something completely different.

If people are bored, give them a task. If people are uncertain, become certain in the resolve that the difficulty can be overcome. We don't have all the answers. However, if team members don't believe the project is possible, then give them a different interpretation or understanding of the situation.

At all times, we need to install the message that we can become more efficient. This enables others to scrutinise their daily tasks and focus on what they need to minimise, how they can save their energy, time and enthusiasm. Give them permission to ask if they don't know how to make the necessary changes. Also, give others permission to ask for reassurance if they feel uncertain. We can be surprised at how much we can minimise in our everyday life and how quickly things can fuel themselves and get out of control. We need to insure ourselves and others against doubts, concerns and anxieties, so that if they do arise they can be dealt with thoroughly and expediently.

Maximise

We will want to maximise some behaviours because they propel us towards our objectives. We do this by recognising, acknowledging and rewarding the behaviours that are useful. Particularly when individuals are prepared to give more, and when the more they give, the better it becomes. This applies to even trivial behaviours because these too build a sense of progression. They are important to every team member. The personal touches always go a long way in showing others our personal integrity because we are taking an interest in what others value and believe in. If we can recognise qualities in another, we can then respond to individuals in a way that allows them to want to give more.

Not everyone is the same, so we need individual strategies to draw the potential out from each team member. Notice when people are doing their best and assist them to go beyond this. People value time, attention and consideration. A manager who services the team builds reciprocation, whereby the team takes on the challenges to succeed.

Having a personalised program of development for each team member allows us to remain focused on what they can gain from the experience, what qualities they need to explore, and what skills need to be developed further. By investing in each individual we can maximise the return for the team. Relationships which have a social component where members can relax and get away from the project is useful. Even just a talk over morning tea about other things allows us to connect with that person and their passions. The more we share, the more we care. We can also offer:

Encouragement for those behaviours and beliefs, no matter how small, which are important such as persistence, commitment, enthusiasm and beliefs of "We can do it" and "You did a great job." While individuals may give up, the team can keep going.

Energy to focus others' attention on being more productive, while reducing unnecessary distractions, so that an individual's time and energy are not wasted.

Opportunities to learn and gain from personally, so that another's experience is one of personal involvement. Recognise the differences that each person brings and the uniqueness they offer to the team. Each aspect is significant in creating a whole project. When people feel of value, they will be more committed.

As managers, we only have one day at a time, so we can maximise our time, energy and commitment. A word or suggestion at the right time, and in the right place, yields a great return. At the end of each day and project, people will ask the questions "Was it worthwhile?" and "Did I get what I expected in return for my investment?". As managers, we also need to ask these questions at the end of each day. Sometimes only with hindsight do we realise what we missed along the way.

Acknowledging others shows we are considering them all the time. Minimise what is redundant. Do this by asking, "What can we do better?", "How can we do this better?" and "Are we getting the most from our time and energy?". The answers, solutions and resources are always there for us, particularly when we continue to ask different questions which challenge our beliefs. This mindset is the basis of common sense. It prepares us for the tough times, where we may have to dig deeper, because the first person we should do this with is ourselves and our own potential.

Case Study

Dave is a skilled family therapist who works with elegance and ease in making families functional again. We all grow up inside a team. This is our family. At times things go really well, and at other times we can have the most amazing dramas. In the process of learning how to work with families there are many things to keep track of. It is easy to be seduced into the problems and give solutions, rather than assisting the system to move on.

Dave's approach to his work has always been to keep it simple. Allow others to make it complex. Keeping things simple allows you to do what you have to do, particularly when facing tough times. His overall approach was to minimise the seriousness that people placed on issues, and to maximise their possibilities and choices. He had a belief that humour was important in releasing the intensity that stopped people from accessing their best attributes and qualities. The quicker you can get people to laugh at their situation, the more likely they are to perceive it differently.

Dave's philosophy when working with families reminded me of one particular case which involved four partners in an accounting firm. All the standard clichés applied. These boys were serious. They had every right to be, accounting was a serious business. If you don't take yourself seriously, who would? But then they started to believe in their own beliefs which were different amongst the group. They were no longer the excellent firm that they had been. All they had to do, however, was to laugh at themselves, and re-connect with their own skills. Minimise the differences, while highlighting them as resources which added to the overall partnership. In other words, they did a personal audit and gave each other a personal value, and then set about how they were to depreciate each other!

Initially they thought this was strange because I told them they hadn't appreciated themselves, so they might as well use their skills to depreciate something. People depreciate 12.5 percent per year, therefore since they had been in the partnership for nearly six years they were close to writing each other off. They all enjoyed the idea of working out how much each was worth. Nothing balanced. They had heavily invested in seriousness and had forgotten about the cash flow of the partnership. A sense of humour and respect for everyone's contributions needed to be added. So they had to draw up new books or put themselves into liquidation.

By keeping it simple and not buying into the power struggle, they were able to re-evaluate the situation and approach it from a different point of view. They are still in partnership because they see the value in each other. Too easily we can learn that seriousness becomes a way of life and people and relationships are the cost. When things get tough we need to minimise the issues and maximise the people.

Transcript

Resolving a project is usually required as the project initially gets underway. At first management has to come to terms with the project and make decisions that count. The difficulties faced at this stage are generally about not having enough resources, people, time, money and whether the project is plausible or not. This is why planning and preparing all team members become vital. At some point during the project there will be a difficulty or a challenge.

Challenges require that individuals not only face their difficulty, but overcome it. It is too easy to get bogged down in content and dramas. In the end, if people spend too much time in histrionics we are actually rewarding and acknowledging this process. Ultimately challenges leave us with questions like "Did we push it enough?" and "Did we go for it?".

Dramas are a product of our society and are a way of gaining attention and importance to the individuals involved. Funny thing is that people don't like them, yet seek them out, again and again. Dramas almost add richness to a humdrum existence. Doing more of the same only ensures another problem will need to be solved, so that the solutions become the problem.

Those managers who take themselves too seriously become fixed and stuck. In the end they have to prove they were right and do so at the expense of the company and the people. In relationships everybody can be right. If we want to fight about something we will, which is sad. We need to ask "How much of the problem am I making?" and "If I was different would this situation still exist, or how would this problem occur differently?"

Those managers who I find most difficult to deal with are those who sit and wait until they are proven right. They don't do anything to assist, they just sit and watch and say "Mark my words!" These people are not team players and are the first people I would sack, because they have resources which they are not using.

It is so easy with hindsight to point the finger. These people lack leadership skills because they are too engrossed in saving face. They need personal resolve and the ability to share their experiences. To face resolve requires taking a risk. Business demands this. We need to save bodies not faces because people are more important and ultimately their learnings are the future business.

The nice thing about taking risks is that it can be creative, especially if we find ourselves with dramas. If this is the case, then we have to be the one creating these effects. This is what we need to work on. If there is something that we are doing and we are taking ourselves too seriously, then resolving it only enhances our potential. So we must be careful of our own patterns and how we impose these on others.

Exercise of Day 5: A Sense of Resolve

Minimising the uncertainty

Usefulness

1. Durability – to carry on through the tough times.
2. Manage stress and tension.
3. To draw and expect more than we thought possible.

Concepts to be Remembered

- Doubts and anxieties are contagious.
- We need to reassure ourselves and others.
- Change is as good as a rest.
- We don't have all the answers.
- Giving permission is very powerful.

Steps

1. Self-analysis: What are your doubts, fears and anxieties? These are the things that we need to manage first.
2. Pick one area that you are uncertain about. What do you need to do to minimise the uncertainty?
3. What do you tend to avoid at work? How could you take on these activities more frequently? (Remember people watch you as a model. They note your prejudgements.)
4. Note your daily habits and minimise them, or display these habits in a new way. (Otherwise, you promote habits and excuses in others.)

What Type of Learning Occurred For You?

☐ Awareness	☐ Skills	☐ Knowledge
☐ Insight	☐ Hindsight	☐ Foresight
☐ Technique	☐ Procedure	☐ Experience

Daily Record: A Sense of Resolve

1. Concepts/abstracts covered.

____

____

____

____

____

____

2. What do you want to use less and what is useful to you after the day's reading? Consider your behaviours, beliefs, thoughts, emotions, self-talk and values, for your own personal development as well as the development of staff and the company.

Personal Development

	Use less	Useful
Behaviours	__________	__________
Beliefs	__________	__________
Thoughts	__________	__________
Emotions	__________	__________
Self-talk	__________	__________
Values	__________	__________

Staff Development

	Use less	Useful
Behaviours	__________	__________
Beliefs	__________	__________
Thoughts	__________	__________
Emotions	__________	__________
Self-talk	__________	__________
Values	__________	__________

Company Development

	Use less	Useful
Behaviours	__________	__________
Beliefs	__________	__________
Thoughts	__________	__________
Emotions	__________	__________
Self-talk	__________	__________
Values	__________	__________

DAY 6: A SENSE OF ACCOMPLISHMENT
The notion of completeness

As we set off on our journey towards our destination, the end in sight is the compelling reason to strive forward. It is not until we reach our destination that we experience that moment of achievement, that sense of fulfilment, satisfaction and relief. If the journey is long and hard then this sense of accomplishment may be a long way off. Therefore, as managers we need to extract along the way all those things which have been accomplished, and there will be many.

Each one of these experiences are invaluable since they fuel and assist the journey. It is up to us to ensure that these accomplishments are acknowledged. Managing a team requires the special task of accomplishing the process of people working together in an enhancing way, rather than one that limits. We have to be able to direct a team from being dependent upon us, through to interdependence on other team members. Along the way we have to acknowledge our individual skills and independence. In working with senior managers recently I asked them what would be the skills an accomplished manager would use to develop a self-managed team. They believed that accomplishment for a manager pertains to not only team performance, but also to the abstractions or relationships experienced by team members. The qualities this group of managers identified fell into three categories. What was important to them was how people related, the position they held, and finally the experiences which were created:

1. How people *relate* – Whether the manager is open, approachable, and a good listener.
2. To do with *position* – Being objective, decisive, and non-judgemental.
3. *Experience* – Awareness, acknowledgment, and consideration.

Then I asked them how many of these factors they experienced themselves. If they had these experiences, how did they rate themselves and what work did they still need to do with them? These are the personal things managers need to accomplish. Life isn't a static event. Instead it is a progression, moving towards our objectives and dreams. Life is also about moments which are so special that they become memories. The older we become, the more the future shrinks away, the more our memories expand.

When we go to work we need to think about which memories we want to keep, and which memories we want to plan for. Being open, approachable and a good listener requires that we be friendly and exhibit consideration for others. We have to put aside our concerns and worries, and at times even our job, to make sure we are valuable enough to those around us. We need to allow others to approach us so they can reach us, if needed. The reason why people don't approach us sometimes is because of our position, rather than our personality. They assume we have enough worries and concerns and don't want to be a burden to us.

Others have an uneasiness with authority figures. Each of us have important figures in our lives. Not all of those have been benevolent and considerate. Being in an authority position requires that we must lead and know what is expected. Unfortunately others may be uncomfortable about how they can relate to us because there is always an underlying set of rules of behaviour which is considered appropriate. So people tend to play it safe to make sure they have our approval. Lastly, others can be in awe of our reputation and ability. People attribute things to others that are not necessarily there. They hear rumours and respond accordingly. Giving time, consideration and personal attention goes a long way to reducing these concerns.

Our position doesn't make us a better person. It just gives us more privileges and power. However, we have far more power when we continually work and strive to earn these privileges, based on our own accomplishments. Befriending people and pursuing their potential may require time and energy, but this builds something which is special. It is ultimately the people who accomplish and complete the project.

The ability to be objective, decisive and non-judgemental are ongoing skills that we have to learn. No two experiences are the same, nor two decisions alike. So each time we are objective or decisive, it is as if for the first time. The only thing we have is experience, knowledge and our skills to draw upon. So every time we are faced with decisions this in itself is an accomplishment. We have so many accomplishments each day that we can often take our own ability for granted.

If we don't acknowledge these accomplishments, we become complacent. Rot sets in. This undermines all that has gone before. In working with people nothing is guaranteed. The decisions we make may not be liked by everybody and we all make mistakes. But we will accomplish something, even if it is not what we intended. Put aside personal likes and dislikes, and be in a state which is conducive and free from strong emotions and private agendas. Lastly, we are paid to make the best decisions based on our experience and knowledge. In doing so, we have accomplished what we can. If we can't do any more, then say so. No one is by any means complete.

Awareness, consideration and acknowledgment are about creating experiences that are worthwhile for others. People know if we are alert and know what is going on in the team. We show this through interest, curiosity and an intrigue for the project at hand. For things we don't know we need to ask questions, seek new information and model wanting to learn for others. When someone shows an interest in us, we usually find this an enjoyable process. It is the same for our team members. All of us need to be acknowledged. It is satisfying when we receive it from others. It can assist us to feel complete.

Being recognised is the first step towards being respected. Showing consideration acknowledges we have thought about someone, which is one of the best ways to give a compliment to another. People thrive in an environment where they feel they have value and thought has been given to them. All it takes is a word of recognition, active consideration and a pertinent question which notices what others fail to see. All these qualities will be paramount while implementing a project, because it is during this time that the team will require more from us. We have the opportunity to lead the way. These are our accomplishments.

Parameters of Accomplishment: Obvious and Elusive

Accomplishments are about appreciating the things that have been done. It is our job to identify and highlight these, for they can become the tools of encouragement, motivation, comprehension and understanding. It will be that sense of accomplishment that will motivate the team to push towards completion. Some accomplishments are obvious, while others are elusive.

Obvious

Obvious accomplishments are tangible, and can be measured objectively. When we find these experiences they need to be emphasised so that they create their own momentum and direction for people to follow. Feedback and 'feedforwarding' information can quickly identify accomplishments throughout the progress of the team. When we mark out useful experiences for others, they are more likely to follow.

Obvious accomplishments can occur within relationships. This area is fertile ground for ensuring the team performs to its full potential. Relationships will include how people give feedback and respond to each other. This is paramount in fostering unity and a strength that only comes from working with others. Connecting with others allows us to become accomplished in giving consideration, recognition and commitment, and showing courage, especially when the project is difficult and the deadlines are stringent. Our relationships within the team give us the opportunity to shine, particularly when others need our support.

Accomplished relationships will include:

Acknowledging achievements

Showing appreciations

Sharing of ideas

Offering suggestions

Challenging the concepts and premises

continued ...

... continued from page 133

Offering understanding to points-of-view

Accepting differences

Taking someone's idea further

Taking a risk on something that might be disagreed with or not liked

Being actively involved in conflict

Assisting and supporting others' mistakes

Looking for answers rather than blaming people or equipment

Asking questions

Making requests and negotiating

Seeking assistance

Being interested in each other

Including others, even if not necessary

Spending time on outside interests

All of the above go a long way in ensuring healthy dynamics. Acknowledging those involved, either verbally or non-verbally with a nod or smile, assist others in utilising resources. They are the essence of building a loyal relationship and a shared sense of camaraderie. People feel included and part of a group.

Obvious accomplishments can also be identified by examining how the project is developing. We can acknowledge when one part of a task is completed, particularly when completed ahead of time or finished in a more effective way. People need to feel secure to take the initiative, and to know that even a mistake can provide an opportunity to learn. As managers we need to become more involved when initiative from one individual may jeopardise the team's integrity. The purpose of acknowledging these everyday tasks is about continuing with a sense of progress and flow. When the team's movement becomes stilted or stuck, it leads to a disjointedness and disorientation which will undo the good work completed so far.

Elusive

Elusive experiences are those that perhaps don't make much sense at the time, and may even be disagreeable to other team members. Difficult decisions have to be made. This is when we may have to show our own resolve and courage, because at times we will not be liked. What we cannot forget is that our team is creating something new. Even when completing routine and familiar tasks, the team still has to create new standards, or else they become stale. It is up to the team leader to get individuals to that level of excellence. How they finally arrive at their destination may not necessarily be obvious to them or even to ourselves at times!

Most of a manager's work is about progress. In other words, we have to think of the overall progress by co-ordinating individuals, rather than becoming caught in the moment 'firefighting' and problem solving. This task is not too difficult. Each individual will be stimulated and motivated by different things. We have to relate and stimulate each person within the team. We can then create something compelling. As a manager, we have to make sense, or translate, in many different ways to facilitate understanding for others. Flexibility and conciseness are crucial at this point, since when we are translating we are speaking another's language.

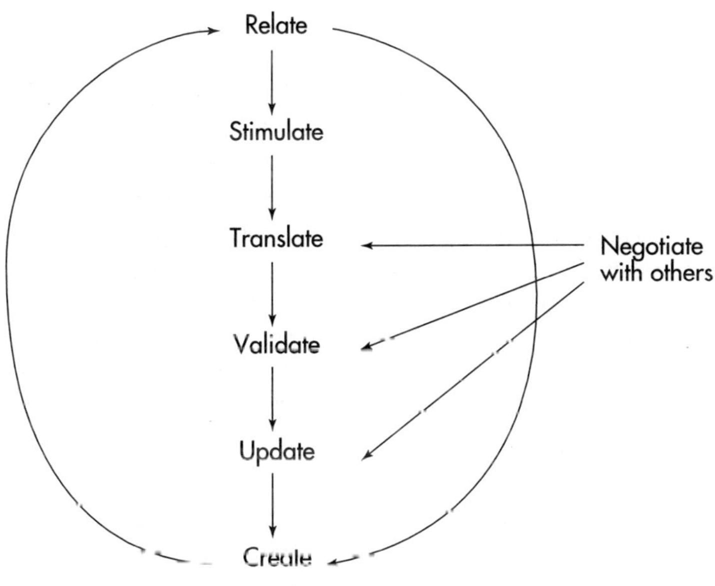

Of course, as team managers we still have the ability to command or demand, and rely upon individuals to trust our judgement. We can ask others to store their resistance away, bear with us a little longer, and deal with the issue at a later date. One of the simplest things to do is to check with others what they mean, to validate whether they have clearly understood. This may seem tedious but it actually saves time in the future.

People can go off on tangents. Because the project is developing we have to update ourselves and other team members to any new developments. People get justifiably annoyed if things are changing and they are not aware of them. Notifying others of the changes occurring allows them to adapt and be more creative in responding to these changes. As a team, the more creative each member can become, the more information we have to relate to.

Acknowledging the accomplishments that are made by the team is about building substance, especially where real risks are taken. In the end, we want a team which has its own identity, with individuals who have a strong sense of self, purpose and function, whose accomplishments outsiders can only admire and respect.

Case Study

One of the best supervisors that I ever worked with was Judy. She was 44 years old, and responsible for projects and operations in a toy company. She had two distinct jobs and ran them both with ease. She never appeared flustered or used worn out excuses, such as, "I don't enough time," or "I wish people could show more initiative." Yet if anybody could use excuses it was her!

Most other companies would employ two people to do her job. So what made her different? It was her approach to work. To begin with, it wasn't a chore. She saw her daily routines as necessities, and each necessity to her was an accomplishment. Therefore, she guaranteed a way to reward herself. She had believed that nothing gets done by talking about it. When talking to her about the difficulties she faced, it became evident that she perceived things differently from most other people.

She wasn't interested in problems. She saw these as challenges to be delegated. What concerned her most was the relationships with her staff who had varied backgrounds. She had a design team that could design the impossible. She had a production team who had to produce the impossible. She had the accountants and administration who demanded the impossible, but a personal resolve that believed if they said it was impossible, then there must be a way. She had an uncanny way of looking at the word "impossible". She broke it down to "I'm-possible" and that was enough!

She would say it was a beginning at least. Knowing where to start was the first hurdle. The rest was making it all come together. Her role was to connect people, resources, ideas and abilities in a way that made things happen. And she had her daily tasks to perform, which she thoroughly enjoyed because it meant that at least she accomplished something.

She had satisfaction at completing even the simplest task. Her real challenge came from creating ways to produce the impossible. When she felt stumped she would distract herself with different relationships and different departments. She had a belief that solutions were inside people waiting to be found, and finding these solutions was her primary purpose.

Judy said she had enough dependence within her own family and children. She didn't come to work to "mollycoddle" people. She wanted them to become reliable, with themselves and each other. When you think about it, it is an enormous task to accomplish. She just said, "Take it one step at a time. I have many relationships with two things in common – myself and the potential of every single person I relate to." She created a desire for people to be part of her challenge. Then together they worked on it. People have their own dreams that they are willing to share. If something doesn't work, do something different. Regardless of what others do, we have to keep on producing and not get drawn into side issues or distractions. If we don't make our own accomplishments, then we can't expect anyone else to either.

Transcript

When we have a list of things to do, it is easy to accomplish. We can check it off as we go and enjoy the list being completed. However, this is only a small part of managing a team. The checklist will get us part of the way, but we need to check our list. What is on it? What is relevant and useful?

Checklist managers are not managers. They are people who want to complete a series of points and believe this is learning. Instead these managers are consumed about being right, usually at the expense of someone else. Checklists are used as a standard and keeping track of chores. As far as accomplishing in relationships and managing the team, they are about as useful as a sneeze in a thunderstorm! But if that is all we have, hold on to it, defend it, but it will quickly become outdated.

Now that may seem a bit harsh but we don't want people to be the same. We want them to accomplish new things for the company. Therefore, we can't treat them as a checklist. After a while people tend to feel used, like a product. So many people worry about the list that must get done. They worry about the things that don't get done, and if it's not on the list, then it doesn't exist.

Step-by-step learning is one way to transfer knowledge. People like techniques. However, it is knowing when and how to apply an action which is more important. It's hard to accomplish in such a vague area. And yet we still pursue a way of categorising people, to predict their every move. All this does is limit our potential and our relationship with others. The more we control the harder it is to relate and get things accomplished. Most of us only pay lip service to the fact that people are unique.

The real challenge in life is dealing with those vague, grey areas where identifying accomplishments are harder to measure. It is tough at times because we don't have all the answers, so we feel as if not much had been achieved. In the end we don't want to complete relationships. Instead we want to take them as far as we can, and create something special; something worthy of an individual who is unique. To do this, we have to reduce the assumptions we make about others.

Translation and validation are occurring every moment within a relationship. When these processes are done with generosity of thought, people gain and feel part of something which they can be actively proud of. Often managers explain instructions four or five times. When it hasn't sunk in, they believe the other person is stupid or slow. The only thing that is stupid is the manager believing that the communication has been effective.

Remember "It ain't happened until it happens." So we need to translate the instruction in a different way, to make sure others have heard our message clearly. That is the accomplishment.

EXERCISE OF DAY 6: A SENSE OF ACCOMPLISHMENT
Chunking

Usefulness

1. Something for everyone.
2. Promoting dreams and hope.
3. Creating new standards.

Concepts to Be Remembered

- The greater the risk, the greater the accomplishment.
- The greater the learning, the greater the accomplishment.
- The greater the challenge, the greater the accomplishment.
- We need to be personal with our staff. Acknowledge them and stimulate, translate, validate and update, so they can create their next accomplishment.

Steps

1. Set 2 personal goals for yourself.

   Set 2 personal goals for your team.

   Set 2 personal goals for your company.
2. Now chunk up and down to show:

   How every personal goal can be incorporated into the company.

   How every company goal can be incorporated into our personal lives.
3 What risks are being taken by each person? How much challenge/stretch are they prepared to take?

4 Chart the last 6 risks you gave taken. What direction are they heading in, are they greater, safer, riskier?

Today

—X—X—X—X—X—X—O—

5. What is the next risk to accomplish?

What Type of Learning Occurred For You?

☐ Awareness ☐ Skills ☐ Knowledge

☐ Insight ☐ Hindsight ☐ Foresight

☐ Technique ☐ Procedure ☐ Experience

Daily Record: A Sense of Accomplishment

1. Concepts/abstracts covered.

____

____

____

____

____

2. What do you want to use less and what is useful to you after the day's reading? Consider your behaviours, beliefs, thoughts, emotions, self-talk and values, for your own personal development as well as the development of staff and the company.

Personal Development

	Use less	**Useful**
Behaviours	__________	__________
Beliefs	__________	__________

Thoughts	________	________
Emotions	________	________
Self-talk	________	________
Values	________	________

Staff Development

	Use less	**Useful**
Behaviours	________	________
Beliefs	________	________
Thoughts	________	________
Emotions	________	________
Self-talk	________	________
Values	________	________

Company Development

	Use less	**Useful**
Behaviours	________	________
Beliefs	________	________
Thoughts	________	________
Emotions	________	________
Self-talk	________	________
Values	________	________

DAY 7: A SENSE OF EXPEDIENCY
The notion of implementation

Most teams are put together to deliver a project. These projects are an enterprise in themselves. They are either about breaking new ground and involving people for the first time, or they are an opportunity to become more streamlined in ongoing work. Planning gets us some of the way, where we target our objectives. Planning involves foresight in selecting the strategies which will allow us to remain focused on what must be accomplished. By doing this the team becomes more efficient and expedient at achieving its objectives.

As the project unfolds, each moment will require insight for the manager to deal and cope with events as they happen. While it's hard to plan for the unexpected, we can expect it to occur. At the end of the project, and after each accomplishment, it is time to extract the learning using hindsight. We become more expedient when we learn from our mistakes, so that they are not repeated when we implement the next project. This assists us in planning our outcome for subsequent activities, since our learning is continually being added to expand our team's resources. There are a number of questions that can assist us in planning and implementing our next project:

1. Did we progress from where we started?
2. Was the project on time and within budget?
3. Did we cover all the aspects?
4. What occurred that we had anticipated?
5. What occurred that we didn't predict?
5. Did the team members live up to our expectations?

In answering these questions, we have to be objective and proportion responsibility to the relevant person. Blame is an easy thing to do, but ultimately this is the responsibility of the manager, rather than external factors or team members. It's too easy to get caught up in cause and effects, which often only leave personal scars.

We need to identify the learning for everyone and focus on what was useful to the team, so that they know what to use less next time. This debriefing should be conducted with the whole team, so that individuals have the chance to finish their business, extract their learning and acknowledge their gains. Debriefing also needs to be delivered individually, so that every person fully appreciates their unique contribution, so that they can add to their own development plan in the future.

Being objective and tactful are the two skills that managers need to consider when facilitating debriefing. When working with individuals they need to be potential orientated, highlighting those behaviours and relationships that worked, while pointing out the reasons why some behaviours didn't enhance their potential. This is the time to set specific individual objectives to incorporate into their behaviour to overcome these shortfalls in being part of the team. People require guidance, so that they can achieve the company's aims and objectives.

When giving feedback, be clear and precise. Keep the highlights and the shortfalls to a minimum of three points; with a maximum of five. Being convoluted, verbose, patronising or condescending is not worthy of the efforts of our team members. Also be considerate of the impact that this feedback may have, and stress the importance of the learning which has occurred. Mistakes are understandable as long as they are not repeated or jeopardise the team or the company. At all times maintain interest in the person, and encourage their involvement in an ongoing relationship. Prepare and plan for the next experience. We should also seek feedback on how effective and expedient we were in assisting others to achieve their aims.

Interventions

We also need to do a personal review of our part in the project. The easiest way to do this is to catalogue the times that we were actively involved in the functioning of the team. This falls into two areas:

1. Intervention in the moment
2. Intervention in the team process

Intervention in the Moment

These are the events where we actively stepped in, or stepped out, of the situation. These are the events which we can use to question our style and our ability to cope. Analyse each of these situations:

- Incident analysis
- Reason for intervening
- Intervention given
- Alternative intervention
- Effectiveness of intervention
- What was gained and what was missed?
- What else could I have done?
- How could it be done more expediently for the next project?

This self discipline can allow us to come up with answers that we can add to the next experience. Ultimate responsibility lies with us to validate the way we responded during the project. Incident analysis assists us in becoming more accountable for our actions. Keep it simple and useful. Build more options at the end of each incident analysis to add to our own development, rather than becoming complacent with the success we have achieved.

Intervention in the Team Process

We need to consider the potential of each team member, and the effect we had on this. What resources are we able to uncover in each person? What can each person do now, that they couldn't have done before? What learning will they take away with them? How have we added to them as a person? The same set of questions need to be asked for the whole team: What was lacking? How would you re-order and prioritise those things that are likely to be useful next time? No two teams are the same, but the resources required will be similar. A project audit will identify how to implement the project more efficiently and expediently next time:

Beliefs: How were beliefs enhanced and limited? Which ones need to be developed for ourselves and the individual team members? Where are their beliefs now?

Strategies: Which strategies were employed to assist people in overcoming their difficulties in relationships? Who can get on well together? Which individuals had the most conflict? Ask each individual, since we will get different responses. What else could we have done with these relationships and individuals? What beliefs got in your way?

Experiences: Did we create the experience in others that we wanted? What happened during the process? How will people remember the project? What experience will they take away? Will our style leave an unpleasant taste, or will it be the achievement and accomplishment of the team? What experiences did they gain? How are they now more experienced, and in what?

Logistics: What wastage of materials occurred? How could this be reduced during the next project? Were all the necessary materials available when they were needed? Was the quality of the materials up to standard? What was overlooked? Was the amount of labour used during the project justified? Will more or less be needed next time? Was the project costed appropriately? Were we above or under budget, and why did these differences occur?

When we conduct a project audit it becomes easier to reinforce the learning which took place during the project, while planning for greater efficiency in the future. Remember, negative experiences are more powerful and they will have a longer impact. Therefore, use them wisely and selectively. Only deliver reprisals when similar mistakes are made frequently, to ensure the lesson is well learned. Always give people a chance to redeem themselves and succeed. One reprisal is not a life description of a person's efforts within the company.

Parameters for Expediency: Industry and Initiatives

The parameters of expediency are industry and initiatives. As managers we need to be in touch and informed on how the project is developing. The best way to do this is to become involved. Honesty is a good policy if we wish to become more expedient, since it gives respect and builds trust in quickly admitting that we do not have all the answers. We also need to intervene and have strategies to relieve the pressure of the moment. When people are tired, lethargic and fatigued, they can't be expected to deliver their best work. They will not be efficient at completing their tasks

Industry

As managers we need to support the whole system. As team leaders our first function is to gather information, and the next is to construct information, to plan. We need to be aware of what matters to us and what's important. The best way to gather information is to get out on to the shop floor and train.

Similarly, the only way to lead is to get on to the shop floor. Different effects can come from this. The most powerful effects will be stepping into the unit, and doing the work. Ask them questions, while at the same time teaching them. Show them the whole process, for instance, "Is this form filled in correctly?" Check that the unit manager knows the standards and expectations. It's not about whether the job was done perfectly. It's about passing on information and working together, building a team.

By doing this, we demonstrate that building a team is important. We show that we are more than just a boss. Explain to those involved what will be occurring beforehand, that working with them is about tracking information, learning what's going on, and what's likely to be needed in the future. We can have a closer working relationship with our staff because we are actually working together with them.

Call an impromptu training. Do ten-minute bursts each day, using a real scenario. This will give not only training skills, but also operational guidelines, particularly in difficult situations. All this builds relationships, collects first-hand data, and promote teams. We can also train in situ. That is, the team watches while the team leader delivers what is required. This builds credibility for the team leader. Ten-minute training blocks will also have a high absorption rate for those watching the procedures. So each day choose something different: ten minutes of what's relevant, and ten minutes of what you think is needed on another day.

Modelling what is required is a way of increasing understanding very quickly. Get in there with them and show them how. Model the process. Repetition builds assurances about getting things right. When there are major changes with staff, get back in there and maintain that essence and energy of the company and the team. Never take for granted that this will always be in place. It requires constant attention.

Initiatives

The other parameter of expediency is initiatives. It is one of the most sought after resources, because new and different actions are created. When we use our initiative we take a risk and put ourselves on the line. This is the enterprise sought after by managers for their workers. However, for initiative to flourish we have to create an environment that's conducive for it to occur. Taking the initiative is a future commodity. Because of its scarcity, it has value.

Initiatives only occur when people feel safe and secure in their abilities, knowledge and in themselves. Team leaders who manage by control or power rarely see this quality in others. Therefore, we need to foster a willingness to learn, with individuals not frightened of making mistakes, but accepting responsibility for the 're-take'. Fun and a sense of humour are the next two ingredients that will make the risk compelling. Once people get to this point they begin to ask questions like "What if this occurred?" or "Where else is this possible?". In other words, we need to become aware of opportunities and openings that occur every day.

People need to be encouraged to take action. Initially this will be fraught with uncertainties and apprehension. How we handle someone who takes the initiative will determine whether other people are prepared to take the risk. Initiative needs to be supported, not chastised. Individuals may not be successful every time, but at least they are involved and everyone has been part of a new learning opportunity.

Taking the initiative requires doing something for the first time, without being told or asked. At the time, it just makes sense. When this occurs individuals are generalising their skills from one context into another area. They have taken their learning and modified or adapted it to suit new needs. This demonstrates people who own their project, and are actively seeking new ways of getting the most from their work, so that the rest of the team will also reap the rewards.

Initiatives which are successful are the quickest ways to get a promotion within the company because it shows others that we have the ability to apply potential. The fact that we are prepared to have a go and risk making a mistake shows we have spirit; that expediency and learning are our intentions.

Case Study

The best example of expediency that I have witnessed is in a man named Peter. He runs the marine transport for a major oil company. He's not a snappy dresser, nor does he surround himself with electronic gadgets to help him do his work. But as soon as you meet him you know he can do the job. All his life he has been a captain running a tight ship. He is not officious, but his manner and personality tell you that he is efficient in everything that he does.

Peter believes that running around never solved anything, while "shifting and moving papers only caused drafts!" But he did know what sailing a vessel was all about. He knew about the energy, when to push, when to pull, when to take the strain and when to let go. He understood what loads the tug was capable of bearing. Safety was always a paramount importance, to protect the men whom he worked with.

Peter liked the idea that other people had potential. So anything that required a specific task or skill he would always delegate. He was particularly good at delegating, and to avoid confusion he would give instructions which were clear and precise; no long-winded explanations. He also found that if he delegated enough single tasks to be done, sooner or later his workers become experienced and competent in their endeavours.

Because he was so expedient Peter was promoted to a desk job, running the whole department. He now had a fleet of boats to run and organise. This meant he had to deal with several individual skippers. He also had to ensure that each time a boat went out that it did the maximum amount of work possible. Peter had the same expectations of all his captains and demanded they deliver above the standards required. His experience made him aware that when you're in charge of a boat you have to keep an eye on many things, you can't just deal with the one task. People's real potential is how to do multiple things at once.

The previous person who had Peter's job had been an administrator who had no idea of how to run a boat, but could run an office extremely well. Yet because of Peter's valuable first-hand knowledge of what he was managing, he reorganised the whole marine department within a month. Previously, there were unnecessary trips out to the rigs as well as too many bosses; the rig bosses, captains and 'land' bosses. Peter designed a new routine for all the tugs. Except in an emergency, all tugs would go out to complete multiple tasks, rather than visiting just one rig. That is, the tugs now had multiple jobs to do and were servicing several rigs in the area, rather than making frequent return trips to the harbour.

Peter produced a 25 percent increase in efficiency in six months. How he did it was his secret, but his philosophy made sense. "There's nothing more unpredictable at sea than Mother Nature. You have to expect the unexpected and be prepared. People are often like that!"

Transcript

Every project should build onto the next. One of the things we have to consider is that the team may have to be dismantled at the end of the project so that all we have worked for and put together now has to come apart. As it comes apart, we want to ensure that each person takes something special with them. They have the learning, the experience and the relationships. If they continue working in the same team, then we have to be extended and stretched further, and the need for a development plan becomes crucial.

Life is the sum total of our experiences, and even though each is different we can build upon what we personally have experienced. We can move towards the things we want and reach out for those things that are just beyond our grasp. To do this we need to be thorough with ourselves, putting ourselves under the microscope. This is a self-discipline which allows us to be mentally, emotionally, and ultimately physically, healthy. The more we can learn from each experience, the more experienced we become. Knowing our strengths and weaknesses allows us to work to our full capacity, and to become more expedient in the future.

Conflict, doubts and worries are the greatest waste of time, effort and energy. They are not productive, unless they are given a direction or a purpose, such as learning how to reduce these debilitating emotions in future relationships and experiences. It is useful to have doubts, as long as we are prepared to have contingencies or alternative perspectives, and the flexibility to acknowledge and work through these possibilities.

From the people around us, we can learn many things. They have abilities and qualities that will test our style and teach us about human nature. If we could learn one thing from each person we meet, we would become amazingly enriched in how to relate to others and move through our world skilfully and with greater ease, because the more skills we have the more flexible we become at dealing with the unexpected. Each day, adopt a specific behaviour or skill for yourself. At the same time we need to acknowledge that we can't do everything ourselves. That's why we choose people for our teams. Together we can support and add to each other when facing any challenge.

We can come through almost any adversity if our personal efforts are based on integrity, discipline, humour and common sense. These are fine principles in achieving expediency as long as they are updated and relevant to those whom we manage. These qualities build fortitude and a personal strength. They can be the common threads through our experiences and relationships that allow us to deal with obstacles and difficulties.

When we are expedient we have the power to produce the results we want. We know what we want, and we take the shortest route to achieve these objectives. This leaves us with more time and energy to pursue other objectives, and our future dreams. Being expedient is the power that guides and assists others, and is the strength that true leaders exude, with every breath they take.

Exercise of Day 7: A Sense of Expediency

Incidents

Usefulness

1. Promotes growth through feedback.
2. Willingness to learn from each other.
3. Process of modelling excellence.

Concepts to Be Remembered

- Feedback needs to be concise and clear.

- Focus on behaviour and the process, rather than the individual.
- Go from not so good to what's done well.
- i) Room for improvement
  ii) Done well
  iii) Done beyond expectation

Steps

1. Complete an incident analysis of a management issue that has occurred in your company (either positive or negative).
2. Focus on the manager's intervention: when, why, what, how and with whom?
3. What led to the intervention? How could the manager have intervened earlier?
4. If the manager hadn't intervened and let the issue run its course a bit longer, what else may have occurred? Who else would have intervened?
5. What is the next risk to accomplish?

What Type of Learning Occurred For You?

☐ Awareness	☐ Skills	☐ Knowledge
☐ Insight	☐ Hindsight	☐ Foresight
☐ Technique	☐ Procedure	☐ Experience

Daily Record: A Sense of Expediency

1. Concepts/abstracts covered.

____

____

____

____

2. What do you want to use less and what is useful to you after the day's reading? Consider your behaviours, beliefs, thoughts, emotions, self-talk and values, for your own personal development as well as the development of staff and the company.

Personal Development

	Use less	**Useful**
Behaviours	______	______
Beliefs	______	______
Thoughts	______	______
Emotions	______	______
Self-talk	______	______
Values	______	______

Staff Development

	Use less	**Useful**
Behaviours	______	______
Beliefs	______	______
Thoughts	______	______
Emotions	______	______
Self-talk	______	______
Values	______	______

Company Development

	Use less	**Useful**
Behaviours	____________	____________
Beliefs	____________	____________
Thoughts	____________	____________
Emotions	____________	____________
Self-talk	____________	____________
Values	____________	____________

Chapter 8

Depending on the Future

Teams are the way of the future. Collectively we can achieve so much more. Teamwork when done well, is more productive and effective than the individual alone. Producing a team which is effective takes more than just collecting a group of people together. It requires that those involved connect and share a vision. They need to do more than their daily tasks, if the team is to excel. When each individual is prepared to give more than the minimum requirements, we have a group who are prepared to support and assist each other in the learning process. They give freely and go beyond their job descriptions. They understand that relationships are all important when working together.

Some individuals prefer to stand alone. They don't function well in teams because they are naturally competitive and will withhold information to maintain their power base and alliances. In fact, many teams do not demonstrate good examples of teamwork, since the group activity is merely an individual forum or sub-groups for subversive and covert politics. These individuals use the team process as a vehicle for personal advancement. Invariably, conflicts will fester and issues will remain largely unresolved. The project may be completed, but the experiences and relationships during the team's activities will be uncomfortable and many will feel unsafe to take risks and express their views openly. Self-protection becomes the primary motivation.

Alternatively, others produce their best achievements when they connect and work with others. They value advancement of the whole team, and no one individual shines. Team members have a shared vision, a purpose that guides their direction. They are all personally committed to the objectives that have been set, and they see the work that they do together as something that really matters. Every player performs a crucial role in reaching the team's destination, and individuals believe that all contribute equally in their own unique way. People feel valued and see no need to waste their energy on self-protection, since the group will provide support and loyalty to all its members. Information will flow freely, while conflict and disagreement is viewed as a healthy process, necessary for encouraging creativity and uncovering a greater variety of options when making decisions. When difficulties do arise, individuals remain focused on the issue, rather than personally criticising team members. Team performance remains paramount; individual egos rate as unimportant.

Teams working effectively together in the future is an ongoing process that requires monitoring and attention to detail. When teams function brilliantly it is not by accident, but by design. Careful planning and being aware of the processes within the team are constantly under the microscope, so that any concerns which may arise are dealt with swiftly before they can grow into major difficulties. The team leader, as well as all individuals within the team, remain focused on the overall vision of what's possible for the groups to achieve. To do this, participants are continually processing the following:

T	=	Towards building a direction in the face of change.
E	=	Effectiveness and efficiency on how to get to their destination.
A	=	Attaining all that's possible from the group experience.
M	=	Management skills and challenges which enhance performance.
S	=	Sharing and supporting each other through conflicts.

W	=	Way finding, exploring what's possible and opening up new ground
O	=	Orientation to the requirements of others and additional options generated.
R	=	Reframing difficulties as challenges to be pursued, with vigour.
K	=	Knowledge and learning that will enrich experiences and create greater wisdom.
I	=	Information shared to develop new ideas.
N	=	Needs monitored and met for the individual as the team progresses.
G	=	Growth of the company and generative strategies to remain successful in business.

The goal of any team is to enhance the company within which it works. A company made up of cohesive 'splinter' groups within the organisation will be counter-productive. The team can never become bigger and more important than the overall system. Instead, all departments and teams support and activate the larger vision, so that the company remains viable. Therefore, no one team is independent of other groups working within the organisation. All have their part to play, and while some teams may be more visible to the public, all teams should see their primary role as providing support for other departments. We all service other employees. When we take this perspective as our creed within our particular team, then the success of the company as a whole remains in focus. Just as personal egos should never dominate team decisions, team or department egos should not predominate over the general welfare of other teams within the company.

It is the responsibility of all employees to appreciate how they individually contribute to the larger system; that each of us is a spoke in the company wheel. All of us bring our own personal qualities, skills, resources, past experiences and future aspirations and dreams into the organisation. We also bring our standards and our confidence and credibility. Above all, we bring with us our level of openness, and attitude and approach to learning. Undoubtedly, all of these factors will have an effect on the company and those who work with us. We are certainly able to make an impact and leave our mark on those who come in contact with us.

Just as we can make an impression upon the course that the company takes in the future, at the same time the company will affect us in a variety of ways. When we take on the sense of purpose and future directions of the organisation, we too are changed. We absorb information, knowledge and attitudes from those around us, and we develop additional skills that assist us in becoming more experienced. This, in turn, will influence our potential, personal growth and development.

Being able to facilitate others and getting the most from and with them will build a potential that will unfold, like watching a child grow. This can be intoxicating, for it's an achievement that continues into the future, rather than goals that have to be reached and reset, again and again. The relationships between the individual and the team and company is therefore a two-way process:

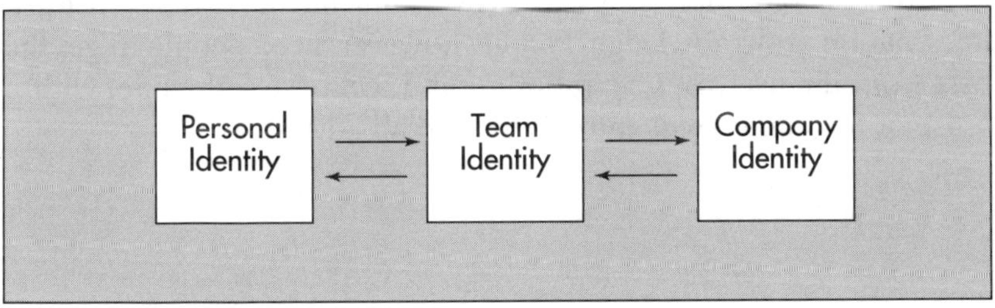

The relationships we experience with our fellow workers can incorporate a range of behaviours, from dependence, independence through to interdependence between teams and departments. We can, of course, move between these three processes, depending on the situation. Individuals need to be dependable, so that we can hand over instructions and know they can go about their work in an independent way. We want to rely on others to do their job without the constant need for checking up on their standards, so that the completion of tasks reflects the standards of excellence stipulated in company policy. We also want individuals to be independent in their thinking, so that more options are generated rather than employees mindlessly following guidelines which may have become outdated.

Smooth operations within the team will occur when individuals are dependent on company protocols to direct their behaviour. However, employees will stay longer with the company if fulfilling their future dreams and personal potential is dependent on the success and growth of the organisation. Similarly, we are interdependent when we exchange ideas and require the support of those around us. This builds relationships of substance and experiences which are rewarding. We connect in a way that is mutually beneficial.

There are times when we want people to stand on their own feet so that they work independently. This can make the best use of resources, time and energy. Quality, quantity and effectiveness of work is determined by team leaders freeing the system to allow individuals the space to express themselves, and room to move so they are more likely to take the initiative in discovering new ways of completing objectives. Managers need to create a structure which is flexible to the needs of people in the company. This will allow their uniqueness to shine through which can add to the team's performance and identity. Employees are then more likely to remain focused and more importantly, seek new ways to deliver and facilitate relationships, information and knowledge. People, however, need people to get the best from themselves. Comradeship and feeling worthwhile, with a sense of belonging, will endure through all adversity.

Company Requirements	Personal	Relationship
Dependent	**Independent**	**Interdependent**
Protocols and rules	Completing tasks	Exchange of ideas
Leader's direction	Thinking and anticipating	Companionship
Company purpose	Creating options	Servicing departments
Team performance	Improving standards	Influencing others
Systems and procedures	Accountability	Giving/receiving feedback
Decisions by the majority	Risk taking	Market trends
Customer support	Personal development	Fulfilling company needs
Government laws	Freedom of choice	

RELATIONSHIPS OF THE FUTURE

All business is based on relationships. We can influence those around us by giving them the space they require so that they feel safe enough to let us into their private world. At team meetings we deliver information through our own 'maps' of the world. For instance, when we decide a colleague is unreliable, our prejudices are activated, so that it is more difficult for us to like this person. Obviously, this will not add to the relationship. Too often we discard individuals, and ignore their potential and ability to grow, based on our own biases and outdated information. We can be quietly powerful and subtle in our approach. Lead by example. We can demonstrate to our team members that we are not quick to make judgments. When our colleagues observe that we treat others with fairness and support, they soon realise that this is also the way they will be treated by us.

Everyone likes to feel special, not only our customers, but also those we work with. When a customer or colleague comes forward, and then retreats, something has been said or done to close them down. If individuals are not coming forward it is likely that we are not inviting them sufficiently to take that initial step. We need to identify what occurred just prior to their shift 'inwards', so we can understand what is likely to stop this person in the future. There are so many ways we can promote people in our company, and it's not just a new title on their office door!

People need to be open and feel safe with us, if they are to be in touch with their resources. They need to be given the space to take risks without the threat of verbal annihilation or sarcasm if they fail. Otherwise we will only receive lip service and platitudes. Companies never grow by continuing to play it safe.

It is important that we are able to move through a working environment that actively supports change, growth and development. Personal change concentrates on re-sequencing behavioural patterns. Personal growth requires adding something to their experiences, while personal development refines these skills and abilities, so their experiences become richer.

Change completely alters past patterns of responding. These patterns are different from then on. Very few people want change because behavioural responses are hard to give up. We do what is familiar, not what is necessarily productive or useful. We unconsciously replicate sameness, stability and security. These are our primary concerns. Adapting to change around allows us to become smarter at what we do. However, we tend to be passive and only notice change when things go wrong. This is a problem-solving orientation. Learning to do things differently, and taking a new perspective allows us to become more creative in the changes that can occur in our relationships.

We can't not grow! All of us are in the process of growth from the day we were born. We grow through our own experiences. They add to who we are, and what we will become. Obtaining a greater variety of experiences benefits, not only ourselves, but those around us. Growth occurs when we have something to strive for, that gives us purpose. This can be in a real sense, such as collecting possessions, or in a qualitative sense, by seeking love, friendship and a sense of belonging.

This purpose gives our existence substance. Through this striving, we accumulate richness and resources, which we can pass onto others. The majority of people need assistance in putting the pieces together. Offering ourselves and our experiences not only enlightens our own understanding, but enriches others with possibilities. All of us are in the process of getting better at what we do. We are constantly developing our skills by refining them, so that we become more effective and efficient. The importance of this process is to take the raw material, and to refine it until it becomes an elegant, admirable quality. It's about making things better. Everything in life is constantly developing, as we seek to fine-tune our abilities even more. It's called experience.

Working with people is primarily to get them to activate all the resources they have, so that they become more skilled at being their own 'change agents'. This, in turn, produces better results. Facilitating people to cope and adapt allows them to become more comfortable and open in facing new challenges and changes. Over time, planning for change and personal growth and development can facilitate our team to excel in the process of working together, in the art of doing

Content *(What will be done)*	**Process** *(How it will be done)*	**Structure** *(Where are the limits)*
For example: A new boss is arriving in the company	How will his style affect the company?	What parameters will he put into place or review?
Change: What will be done?	How will he do it?	What reference points will be put into place during implementation?
	Can the task or decision be re-sequenced?	

	Content (What will be done)	Process (How it will be done)	Structure (Where are the limits)
Growth:	What new learning experiences will be added to the company?	Are there better ways to make sure the change happens?	How can we increase our strategies and ways of doing things?
Development:	What has to be refined for implementation?	How do we deliver the change with greater precision?	How do we monitor the implementation for efficiency, such as reduced paperwork?

business. When implementing a new decision within our company, our team can consider the possibilities below, as a way of organising what needs to be monitored:

To utilise the notions of change, growth and development more fully, we can present the following questions to our colleagues within the team at our next meeting:

- If you could change something about the company, what would it be?
- If you could change something about yourself, what would it be?
- If you could add something to the company, what would it be?
- If you could add something to your personal repertoire, what would it be?
- If you could develop or shape something further in the company, what would you refine?
- If you could develop or shape something further in your personal development, what would you refine?

Scrutinise these answers carefully, since they will give us invaluable insight into the needs of our colleagues:

- What have you learned about each member of your team?
- How can you and the company assist this person to achieve their needs?

We should give feedback to our group about how their comments have been genuinely considered, and what measures will be implemented to satisfy, as best we can, their requests. Be seen as someone who cares, someone who listens and someone who does!

Remember that we are all on a learning curve. This curve, however, is different for each of us. New members to the team will be on a high learning curve, while still establishing relationships and gaining experiences. By comparison, those individuals who have been with the company a long time are likely to have entrenched and meaningful connections with their work mates, and to have wide experience in the work that they do. However, they run the risk of doing things the way that they were always done, so their learning curve may have plateaued!

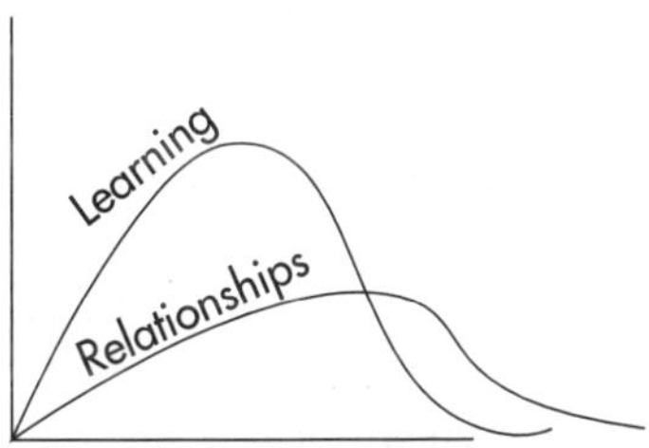

New Employees

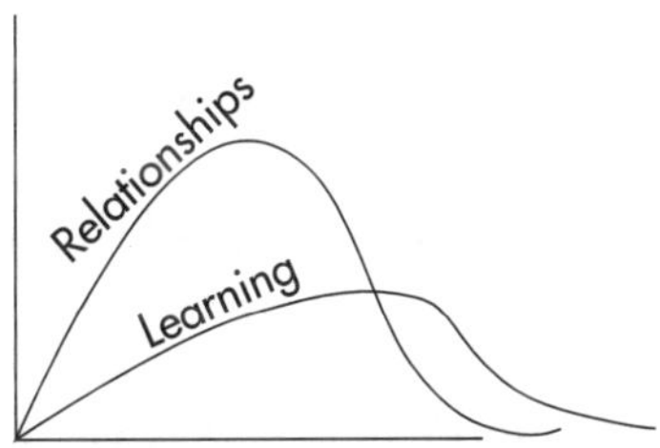

Established Employees

Everyone has something to add. Provide the space that encourages contributions from everyone. It's too easy to cut people off in their prime. The inexperienced can provide a freshness and a new approach particularly in the latest technology, while those fully initiated in the company's system can add a rich dimension or wisdom that only experience can provide.

Building new relationships requires testing unfamiliar ground and establishing the rules. Take a look around your office, and notice the relationships. A business relationship can still be warm and friendly. See every client or customer as a possible friend in the future. It changes the way we do business! Create an opening and build a connection that results in a deeper bond and a more solid foundation. If we leave it too long, the opening will close down naturally.

Creating this opening for others must first begin with ourselves. That is, become more receptive and approachable. Freedom from past patterns of responding requires taking a small step in doing things differently. We can provide support for those around us by noticing how they conduct their business. For instance, a good receptionist creates openings and is inviting to all those who come into the waiting room. Invariably, her posture is extending and welcoming. Her personal space or energy encompasses the entire reception room. This is her space, and like a hostess having a dinner party, she is concerned about people feeling comfortable and at ease. Similarly, the effective personal assistant will protect her boss at all costs. She can be relied upon to buffer any irrelevant distractions, and she is particularly cautious and perceptive when giving out information. Outsiders will have to get past her first, since the well-being of her boss is paramount. She is always polite and respectful, but still has the ability to close down unwanted interference that may distract. Loyalty is the key.

Team leaders encourage, supervise or direct what work has to be completed. There will be times when they need to be authoritarian. Each leader does this differently. Observe the manager who adds to the employee's experiences, so that the team is productive and efficient, yet members feel safe to give their suggestions on how to do things better. Good managers have to provide their own support, since there will be times when they need to be tough, when they will stand alone. Maintaining personal integrity is going to be crucial when making these hard decisions.

We can learn from those around us. For instance, we can select five individuals whom we work with, and notice how they interact with others. We can then identify what we can learn from these individuals that will improve how we relate to those around us. Remember, each person's 'map' is a chance for us to explore. Every map is really a treasure map. It is built upon a wealth of experience, because everyone has their story to tell.

Chapter 9

Pointers to Better Team Management

Being part of a team, as with our families, provides us with the exquisite possibility of connecting with others, building relationships and learning from others' experiences. People are social animals. We enjoy being part of a larger structure where we belong and where our contributions are considered worthwhile.

Within crowds we lose our identity and our uniqueness. Decisions are not paramount and there is little sense of accomplishment. Teams, however, allow us to move toward a common goal. We share expectations. We share our success and achievements, as well as our failures and difficulties. Together, we can accomplish so much more than an individual alone. Teams can develop our potential, stretch our abilities and add to our resources. They are an extraordinary opportunity for us to excel. With a sense of unity and clear future objectives, anything is possible.

The challenge when managing teams is to fully utilise all available resources and bring out the best in individual members. To develop cohesion, personal egos need to be put aside for the greater gain. Identifying the function of the team, reducing distractions, staying on course, respecting the differences in opinions and perspectives all require diligence and flexibility. However, there probably is no greater reward than the quiet achiever who leads their team to victory.

The 14 parameters discussed make the job of managing a team easier. They provide a framework which can focus our energy, so that we expediently move towards our objectives.

With a sense of yearning, we want more. We have a desire to go beyond and begin something new. This yearning will sustain us through the difficult times. The job of the manager is to utilise more emotions and beliefs which will assist individuals through to completion.

The Parameters

Sense of		Parameters		
Day 1	Yearning	Emotions	⟷	Beliefs
Day 2	Purpose	Propelling past	⟷	Compelling future
Day 3	Readiness	Oganisation	⟷	Astuteness
Day 4	Involvement	Active	⟷	Passive
Day 5	Resolve	Minimise	⟷	Maximise
Day 6	Accomplishment	Obvious	⟷	Elusive
Day 7	Expediency	Industry	⟷	Initiatives

Believing in the purpose of the team makes motivation easier, as members work towards their objectives.

Just wanting more, however, is not enough. Team members need to be prepared and ready for the part they have to play; also ready for unexpected contingencies. When individuals become actively involved mistakes or errors in judgement may occur, but at least team members are prepared to contribute and take risks, rather than passively wait for direction.

During times of confusion or repetitiveness personal resolve and durability will be crucial. Do not be distracted by irrelevancies. Maximise and reinforce accomplishments while minimising those frustrations and annoyances which do not directly assist in fine-tuning procedures. This is imperative for effective implementation of the projects requirements and for a smooth journey towards task completion.

Many of the accomplishments that can be achieved by a team are indeed elusive. Certainly we can measure whether the project was successfully completed and our targets are met within the stipulated time frame. However, we gain so much from being part of a team. For instance, through others we learn. The more we expose ourselves to a diversity of beliefs, values and attitudes, the faster we can include these different perspectives into our own repertoire. It is the interaction with others that allows us to sift and sort what is useful, delete what is outdated or irrelevant, and absorb what we believe will add to our experiences and relationships. Learning will always be more expedient when we are able to test our viewpoint with others. We can be influenced by others, and we, in turn, can influence.

We have more power and strength being part of the collective. We can also become more creative as we 'spin off' ideas around us, with other members keeping the momentum going. Above all, if energies are focused and distractions reduced, teams represent the most functional way of allocating tasks and responsibilities. The quantity of your work multiplies significantly.

Quality control can be ensured by procedural guidelines. While we share the responsibility, we also share the joy of achieving and a sense of well-being, particularly when completing a project which was difficult. When we persevere as a group we have a common bond and purpose. We have meaning in what we do. We feel involved and we belong. Surely, this is the essence of what life has to offer.

Index

About the Authors

GARY YARDLEY is an international trainer who works with management all over the world. He challenges the limitations of individuals and systems, so that new experiences can be created, and services designed to face the next century.

He draws upon a variety of skills and experiences, and uses some of the concepts from other disciplines. Some of these include training in Neuro Linguistic Programming, hypnosis, counselling, and systems analysis. His forte is in creatively designing new fields of endeavour, such as Personal Space and its applications within the business world.

He is the creator of Experience Orientated Management, which he teaches to increase effective people management, improve sales performance, enhance customer service, produce cohesive and competent teams, and provide a framework for change to be implemented within organisations, smoothly and efficiently.

He works with all levels of management, and acts as an individual trainer and personal consultant to CEOs and general managers, to design and implement future possibilities. He is based in Melbourne, Australia.

JAN KELLY is a psychologist and certified trainer of NLP. Jan designs and presents specially tailored in-house training programmes for government departments and private companies. Her expertise is in group dynamics, combining NLP and psychology, to teach and build pragmatic skills for successful teams.

Jan has been conducting training seminars for the last 18 years, and has presented to the most challenging groups, including angry and disruptive teenagers in residential care, long-term work-care and unemployed, and de-motivated and disillusioned employees who have lost their sense of purpose for the work that they do. Her areas of interest include motivation, stress management, presentation skills and maintaining high levels of energy to increase productivity and achieve personal outcomes.

Gary Yardley and Jan Kelly can be contacted at:

Tenfold Executive Training Pty. Ltd.
85 Barkers Road
Kew, Melbourne 3101
Australia
Tel: (613) 9 853 3417
Fax: (613) 9 853 5985

Gary Yardley can also be contacted at:

Executive Training Approaches
10 Anson Road
International Plaza
Singapore 0207
Tel: (65) 223 3362
Fax: (65) 221 5652

Titles in the Times Business Series

7 Days to Top-Notch Customer Service by Gary Yardley and Jan Kelly

7 Days to Optimum Sales Performance by Gary Yardley and Jan Kelly

7 Days to Effective People Management by Gary Yardley and Jan Kelly

7 Days to Rewarding Change by Gary Yardley and Jan Kelly

Making Powerful Presentations Using Neuro-Linguistic Programming by Gary Yardley and Jan Kelly

Business Confidence: Unleash the Power of Your Personal Space by Gary Yardley

How to Write a Winning Business Plan by Douglas Bullis

How to Invest in Stocks and Shares by Robert Chia and Doreen Soh

How to Invest in Commodities, Gold and Currencies by Doreen Soh

The Complete Asian Report Writer by Graham Colin-Jones

The Complete Asian Letter Writer by Graham Colin-Jones

Contract Law: A Layman's Guide by Catherine Tay Swee Kian and Tang See Chim

Your Rights As a Consumer by Catherine Tay Swee Kian and Tang See Chim

Buying and Selling Your Property by Philip Motha and Catherine Tay Swee Kian

Thais Mean Business by Robert Cooper

Money and Marriage: Family Finance by Margaret Allen

Let's Talk Money by Margaret Allen

Protect Yourself: Your Guide to Insurance Coverage by Doreen Soh